Brief Lives:
Jane Austen

Brief Lives:
Jane Austen

Fiona Stafford

ET REMOTISSIMA PROPE

Brief Lives
Published by Hesperus Press Limited
4 Rickett Street, London sw6 1ru
www.hesperuspress.com

First published by Hesperus Press Limited, 2008

Designed and typeset by Fraser Muggeridge studio
Printed in Jordan by Jordan National Press

ISBN: 978-1-84391-906-3

Contents

Introduction

'What did she say? Just what she ought, of course. A lady always does.' When Emma finally discovers Mr Knightley's true feelings, after forty-eight chapters of misunderstanding, the relief is almost overwhelming. At last, perfect happiness is in prospect, and the joy that arises from the page is all-encompassing. Any sympathetic reader must share the pleasure of the moment when the barriers crash down and the truth is revealed at last, though there is still a sense, even then, of something withheld. Confusion may be gone, but control is not. The tact with which Jane Austen preserves her heroine's privacy, while inviting readers to participate in her intense delight, is characteristic of her mature novels. Of all writers, she is the most adept at creating characters who seem to possess an independent existence *and* a narrator to whom readers feel able to turn as if to an intimate friend.

Emma's reply to Mr Knightley, which is 'just enough' to prompt him to say more himself, is typical of her creator's method. Jane Austen frequently offers the kind of detail that encourages her readers to allow their imaginations free rein, without issuing a subsequent rebuke. *Northanger Abbey* more or less requires us to imagine a suitable husband for Elinor Tilney, when the narrator, conscious that 'the tell-tale compression of pages' means the story is rapidly coming to a close, announces that any detailed delineation of Elinor's husband is unnecessary because 'the most charming young man in the world is instantly before the imagination of us all'. As so often, we are left knowing everything – and nothing. Her narration is at once intimate and elusive, inviting and in retreat. No wonder, then, that so many readers over the years, who have responded to the promise of her fiction with such gratitude, have found themselves wanting to know more about the woman behind the works.

When it comes to Jane Austen's own life, the same enticing balance between intimacy and distance is apparent. We know exactly where she lived and died, and when and where she wrote her great novels. She is surrounded by a virtual forest of family-trees, and the first-hand recollections by her various relations are always the starting point for any biographical research. We can identify her friends and the social circles in which she moved, the homes that she visited and the parties she attended. Letters survive from Austen herself, packed with details about her clothes, her food, her trips away, her needlework, her visitors and her reading. Compared with many writers living two centuries ago, we know a great deal about Jane Austen. And yet, there is still an extraordinary elusiveness about her life. Even though the first biography was written by her brother within months of her death, our knowledge of Jane Austen seems minimal in the areas which really matter – her methods of composition, her education, her political views, her religious beliefs, and above all, her love life. There is some evidence relating to each of these important areas, but all too often, the surviving details seem to throw up as many puzzles as they solve. Like Mr Knightley in the shrubbery, Austen's biographers seem to receive just enough from the object of fascination to make them want to say more. Every reader feels that in some sense, he or she knows Jane Austen. The engaging tone of her narration, the quick truths and deep understanding of human nature are all so distinctive that we seem to recognise her clear voice instantly. Hence the confidence with which so many have been quick to create their own images of the author.

Whether speculation about Jane Austen by her immediate and extended family, or by later enthusiasts, scholars or film-makers, comes close to the original truth is, however, impossible to determine. 'Seldom, very seldom, does complete truth belong to any human disclosure; seldom can it happen that something is not a little disguised, or a little mistaken.' Jane Austen may have had Emma in mind when she wrote this, but it serves as a suitably witty warning to anyone attempting to narrate her own life. The kindness with which Emma's misunderstandings are ultimately treated nevertheless suggests that Austen herself might have derived amusement rather than alarm from the efforts of her followers, and seen that biographical endeavour is always inspired by the intangible attractions of her novels. Her own practice as a writer was to set out situations or intro-duce characters with remarkable economy, leaving the task of drawing out the likely consequences to her readers. It is perhaps appropriate, then, to consider not only the known facts about her life, but also some of their implications.

As soon as the novels are seen not as autonomous worlds, peopled by their own distinct cast of characters and internal rules, but rather as the compositions of a real woman in a particular place and time, questions spring up about the rela-tionship between the life and the writings. Once it dawns on us that Jane Austen's life spanned one of the most turbulent periods of world history, that the American War of Independence broke out when she was six months old, that the Bastille was stormed when she was thirteen, that war between Britain and France went on almost uninterrupted throughout her adult life and that she died within two years of Waterloo, then the silence of her novels on such matters comes as something of a surprise. She was a wartime novelist and yet her writing conjures up worlds in which all the important action takes place on the dance-floor, in the drawing room or the garden. During her lifetime, Britain experienced massive social and economic transformation, with new industrial and agricultural methods of production, urban growth and improved systems of communication developing under the rule of an unstable king and dissolute prince. Uprisings in Ireland, riots in England, victories and losses abroad, political Union, the assassination of a prime minister, all took place while Austen was writing, but none of these public events seem to make much impact on her apparently realistic novels. Why not?

It is not just the absence of contemporary political references that provides a puzzle for readers, however. Once the focus shifts to Austen's own immediate experience, the gap between what is known of her life and what is apparent in her fiction is again clear. Apart from short visits to friends and family, thirty-four of her forty-one years were spent in the English county of Hampshire, and yet none of her novels is set there. She grew up in a household of six boys and two girls, but in her novels she created families of daughters – the Dashwoods, the Bennets, the Wood- houses, the Elliots. Only two of her heroines have an elder brother, even though Jane Austen had five. Her father was Rector of the parish where she was born, but the most memorable clergymen in her novels are absurdly vain, self-seeking figures. She lived with her mother until her own death, but in her novels, the heroines' mothers are either dead, absent or distinctly un- helpful. The Austen family suffered its fair share of illness, death and difficulty, but none of the circumstances quite matches the problems depicted in her fiction. Jane Austen never married, and yet each of her novels adopts the traditional resolution of comedy and fairytale, moving towards it with unswerving conviction.

What are we to make of this? How can we make sense of Austen's life and art? At a time when most women received so little formal education and none could obtain a place at univer- sity, how did Jane Austen come to write books that would command the attention of some of the most brilliant minds ever since? Why were these the novels that Charles Darwin knew by heart? That Tennyson preferred to seventeenth-century polit- ical history? That Winston Churchill read during the Blitz? Such questions require more extensive answers than a short biography can hope to provide, but they are worth considering at the outset because so much of Austen's public persona is still hidden under the modest exterior originally presented by her siblings, and preserved by her Victorian nephews and nieces. The brief life that follows has no interest in tearing down the images of Jane Austen that have been created by numerous earlier admirers and iconoclasts, and to which each new biographer is indebted. It is, however, propelled as much by the puzzles as by the biographical evidence, and sustained throughout by an undiminishing sense of wonder at the fact of Austen's fiction.

As with so many real lives, Jane Austen's did not conform perfectly to the narrative patterns that inform her novels. The reason that she is the subject of this and so many other biographies is that she wrote six fine books. Since they were all published in the space of six years, between 1811 and 1817, this biography is shaped accordingly. If the number of words and the number of years represented do not seem to match, it is because Jane Austen's greatest achievement was packed into less than a fifth of her life. Though rarely placed in the company of her brilliant contemporaries, Jane Austen was just as much the Romantic genius as Keats, Shelley or Byron – full of youthful exuberance, intensely creative once she had found her individual voice, and dead before she reached middle age.

Childhood
1775–87

There are not many babies in Austen's novels. Late in *Pride and Prejudice*, Mr Collins brings news of a 'young olive-branch', which will make the Bennet family's eventual loss of Longbourn complete, while in *Emma* the child to be born at Randalls is perceived by the heroine as the final stage of Mrs Weston's removal. Young mothers tend to be kept largely at a distance from the action, or used for purely narrative purposes, as when the news of Mrs Price's desperation over her ninth lying-in sparks the storyline of *Mansfield Park*. Although we have glimpses of a more kindly attitude in Emma's drawings of her baby nephew, or in Mr Palmer's secret fondness for his son and heir in *Sense and Sensibility*, no young child emerges as a fully rounded character in any of her novels. Judging from comments in her own letters, Austen's views on birth were decidedly mixed. Though a much loved aunt, her private opinion of her own niece, Anna Lefroy's, frequent pregnancies suggests that successive children were not always greeted with delight: 'Poor Animal, she will be worn out before she is thirty. – I am very sorry for her'.[1]

Austen herself had no children, and nor did her sister, Cassandra. Neither did she have much opportunity to play with baby siblings from an early age, unlike so many children of her time. Her eldest brother, James, for example, had the experience of seeing five young baby boys, and two little girls, appear in his mother's arms by the time he was fourteen years old. For Jane, however, the only younger brother was Charles, who arrived when she was three. Mrs Austen's practice was to send her babies to be nursed in the village after their first few weeks at home, so among young Jane's earliest memories would have been the arrival and subsequent departure of little Charles. By the time she was ten, her glamorous cousin, Eliza de Feuillide and her baby son, Hastings, were frequent visitors at the Austen family home, but the little boy's serious health problems meant that he was always a focus of protective anxiety rather than a spring of pure delight. It was not until the next generation of Austen children began to arrive, with the birth of her nieces, Fanny and Anna, in 1793, that Jane had much close contact with babies. And at that time, she was seventeen, and more preoccupied with plans of her own.

Jane Austen grew up surrounded by big boys. Born at Steventon Rectory in Hampshire, in December 1775, she was the seventh child of the local Rector, George Austen, and his wife, Cassandra. When Jane arrived a month late, during one of the hardest winters of the century, Rev. and Mrs Austen were already the parents of James, George, Edward, Henry, Cassandra and Francis. The arrival of another child was therefore not as momentous as births often seem, even though this baby would eventually become one of the most remarkable writers in the English language, and the popularity of her work would ensure the lasting fame of the entire family. As the youngest girl, Jane inevitably developed a sense of herself in relation to her older brothers, to whom she must have turned at different times for help, information, amusement and comfort. The boisterous company meant that her early life was neither quiet, nor dull nor lonely, but it must also have provoked the occasional disappointment, frustration and feeling of inadequacy, as large families invariably do. Among siblings, deep affection and aggravation generally go hand in hand. The reassuring closeness may also have brought dim fears of insignificance – little Jane mattered very much, but still she was only one of eight. As a child, Jane Austen must always have felt that there was someone a bit older and wiser than herself, to provide a model but also, no doubt, to make her eager to prove her own ability.

When it came to talents, her family were not, after all, under-endowed. Her eldest brother, James, born in 1765, was bright, energetic and widely read. He hunted and wrote poetry with equal enthusiasm, a combination of interests less surprising then than now. Edward, three years younger than James, was good-looking and good-humoured, with a steady head and a talent for telling amusing stories. His younger brother, Henry, handsome, clever and rich in optimism, livened up every gathering with his effervescent humour and sparkling conversation. Cassandra, the first daughter, born in 1773, was eighteen months younger than Henry, but more like Edward with her dark beauty, kind nature and quiet intelligence. Francis, who arrived a year later, was active and determined from the start, as evident in the story of him buying a pony at the age of seven to enable him to go hunting with his older brothers. Francis was the first Austen to go to sea, and ended up as Admiral of the Fleet, the highest ranking officer in the entire British Navy. Charles, the baby of the family, born in 1779, was as intelligent, good-tempered, and courageous as the rest, and followed Francis into the Navy in 1791, just before France declared war on Britain. Only George seemed to have missed out. The second son, born only a year after James, was destined to be something of an exile from the family hearth. From childhood, he suffered from fits, speech difficulties and an unspecified mental disability, which led to him being fostered by a nearby family, and largely edited out of the Austen family narrative.[2]

As a child, Jane Austen was part of a family that provided all the security of connection and continuity, but also instilled an awareness of separation and perpetual change. With such a lively family, there was constant amusement, intellectual stimulation and companionship, but only very rarely would everyone have been living under the same roof. The span of fourteen years between the births of the eldest and youngest Austen meant that James was already setting off for Oxford in the year that Charles was born. George's strange exclusion must also have heightened his sister's sense of the lottery of human existence, and the fragility of her own place in a world where one child can be blessed with grace and ability, another with neither. Gratitude for good health and natural gifts, as well as compassionate understanding of those afflicted with difficulties, formed part of Jane Austen's psyche from the earliest years – and informed the novels she would write in later life.

In addition to George's absence, she also had to contend with some abrupt departures. When she was only eight, Edward was adopted by a wealthy, but childless, relative of his father's, Thomas Knight of Godmersham Park in Kent. From Mr Knight's point of view, the action was very generous: relieving his second cousin from the expense of educating at least one of his numerous sons, and guaranteeing the boy a secure future with a gentleman's estate and social standing. Unlike Francis and Charles, who had to earn their place in the world by entering a dangerous profession and working hard to impress their commanding officers, Edward's prosperous future seemed to have appeared from nowhere, as a reward for nothing more than a healthy constitution and position as a younger son (though not too much younger). Once again, the arbitrary but profound differences in people's lives must have made a deep impression on his sister. The wrench of separation also demanded strategies of psychological self-defence, and contributed perhaps to a fear of relying too heavily even on those who were most dear to her.

When Frank followed Edward out of the family home in 1786 to train as a naval officer, the same feelings of loss were compounded by anxiety. The hazards facing a young Midshipman did not require an imagination as vivid as Jane Austen's to provoke the most profound fears, and so when the twelve-year-old boy went cheerfully away to serve King and country, his sister must have wondered whether she would ever see him again. Proper pride in Frank's courage and sense of patriotic duty demanded considerable effort to muster in such circumstances. By the time Charles followed Frank's example in 1791, the fifteen-year-old girl was faced with an even harder task of waving off her little brother into military service just before the outbreak of a war in which naval battles were to prove crucial to the British campaign.

Not all the fraternal exits were quite so traumatic, however. James and Henry both went up to Oxford and came home safely and regularly. James and Edward both enjoyed extensive continental travels, returning unscathed and full of news of foreign countries. The return of any of the sons was a major event at the Rectory, not only bringing the natural joy of reunion, but also a vital infusion of ideas and stories from beyond rural Hampshire. For although Steventon and the surrounding parishes were full of other large families with their own share of births, marriages, deaths and human incidents, there were inevitably times when the tiny village seemed rather quiet. The cycle of the seasons created the natural pattern of the year, while the Church calendar guided the regular services given by Rev. Austen and attended by his family. Life at the Steventon Rectory was measured by the annual Christian festivals – Epiphany, Lent, Easter, Whitsun, Trinity, Michaelmas, Advent, Christmas – as well as being marked by the yearly challenges of the farm and field – ploughing, drilling, lambing, haymaking, harvesting, partridge shooting, foxhunting.

In a rural community, the vagaries of the English weather are particularly important, and since George Austen had a farm to run as well as his responsibilities as a minister of the Church, the conditions determining good and bad harvests were more than just a matter for conversation. For a little girl, however, the changes in the seasons mainly brought different clothes and activities. During the cold, dark winters, once the excitement over the beauty of frosted cobwebs or a sudden deluge of snow had faded, it must have seemed a lifetime before the days started to lighten and last longer once again. Sewing samplers, reading books and playing games could pass the time quite happily, but anything that broke into the frozen months between October and March was very welcome indeed.

When James, the pioneer of journeys into the wider world, came home for the vacation in 1782, he threw himself into amateur dramatics. Oxford had put him in touch with contemporary fashion, and one of the enthusiasms sweeping eighteenth-century England was the vogue for private theatres. The Steventon Rectory might not be as capacious as some of the country houses where miniature versions of London playhouses were being installed, but it had a sizeable parlour and a barn, so why not a makeshift stage? Unlike the Bertram family in *Mansfield Park*, the Austens were fortunate in having parents who encouraged their children's creative talents, and thus constituted an audience rather than an obstacle. Mrs Austen may have been given to spending time on the sofa, like Lady Bertram, but she was also a very lively woman, with a real facility for witty verses, who shared her delight in wordplay and comedy with her children. George Austen was a highly educated man, a Fellow of St John's College before his marriage, who remained keen to maintain his wide intellectual pursuits and literary enthusiasms as well as to nurture the budding ability of the next generation. In order to help make ends meet, as his family grew larger and larger, he offered rooms and private tuition to young gentlemen. Often his pupils went home in the holidays, but those who were still in residence provided the possibility of a larger cast for the family theatricals. Among the earliest productions at Steventon was a tragedy called *Matilda*, in which one of the residential students, Thomas Fowle, who would later propose to Cassandra, read the Epilogue. Mostly, however, the plays offered opportunities for the Austens themselves to showcase their talents and have a lot of fun.

It must have been very exciting for Jane to watch her older brothers performing Sheridan's hilarious new comedy, *The Rivals*

(1775), and to be introduced so early to the memorably muddled Mrs Malaprop, and to Lydia Languish, whose imaginative world so completely eclipsed the real one. Jane was both an integral part of the family and yet also an eager observer, by virtue of being too young to be given a role. She would have enjoyed the final production, but also witnessed the hours of preparation that went into such an ambitious play – the boys learning their lines, rehearsing scenes, setting up props and developing their stage accents. To produce a convincing fiction for a single evening, vast effort, time and co-operation were required. But it was well worth it. For here was a chance to delight a sympathetic audience, to make people laugh, and to demonstrate personal abilities. The plays at Steventon gave James Austen the chance to recite his own compositions alongside those of the best play-wright of the age, a thrilling idea for his exceptionally talented little sister. On the stage, new identities could be assumed and anything seemed possible – a point especially evident in *The Rivals*, where the actor playing Jack Absolute had to play Jack playing Ensign Beverley. Jane would have been laughing, but also learning, because the very idea of a pretend persona was out of the question in the kind of community where everyone had known everyone else since birth. This was a world complete in itself, and operating according to the playful internal logic of Sheridan's drama. The theatre at Steventon, though only a family affair, demonstrated to the younger Austen children just what art could mean, even in the most confined and remote places.

The scripts chosen by James for family performances offered both entertainment and education. For the young Jane Austen, however, observation of the human interactions involved during the periods of rehearsal must have been just as instructive. One person's eagerness to dominate the stage, another's reluctance to participate, endless disputes over casting – all the details that are so well observed in *Mansfield Park* were in evidence at Steventon during her childhood. When Eliza de Feuillide entered the scene for the Christmas production of 1786, the atmosphere intensified as the usual tiffs and reconciliations also took on a decidedly flirtatious edge.

Eliza was the daughter of George Austen's sister, Philadelphia, who had taken the bold decision of risking a long sea journey and tropical climate, when she went out to India in 1752. Once there, she met and married Tysoe Hancock, and eight years later, gave birth to Elizabeth. When Eliza returned to Europe and married the French aristocrat, Comte de Feuillide, she called their son Hastings, after her godfather, Warren Hastings, the Governor General of India and a close friend of her parents, especially her mother. Whether Warren Hastings was actually the little boy's grandfather has often been debated, but the evidence on either side is patchy. Whatever Eliza's parentage, she certainly made an exotic addition to the male-dominated household at Steventon when she swept in to stay for extended visits during the 1780s. Brought up in India, she was familiar with lands that the Austens had only read about. Married to a French Count, she had moved in circles they had only imagined. With her young son and distant husband, she seemed both vulnerable and emancipated. Though some years older than all her Austen cousins, she was young enough and beautiful enough to seem very exciting indeed.

Eliza was not only prepared to join in the family shows, but even to take the leading role in comedies, which meant that the scope for plays – and playing – increased dramatically. The epilogue written by James for Susannah Centlivre's comedy, *The Wonder*, which Eliza delivered in the 1787 production, is basically a celebration of women, and their new freedom from male tyranny:

But thank our happier stars, those days are o'er,
And woman holds second place no more.
Now forced to quit their long held usurpation,
These men all wise, these Lords of the Creation!

To our superior rule themselves submit,
Slaves to our charms, & vassals to our wit;
We can with ease their every sense beguile,
And melt their resolutions with a smile.[3]

It was quite a change for the Austen brothers, and a startling shift of emphasis for the little sisters. Henry was especially beguiled by his captivating cousin, and their enjoyment of each other's company was obvious to everyone. Eliza was ten years older than Henry, and married. By 1797, when he reached twenty-six, however, she had been left a widow and was therefore free to become his wife.

Jane's cousin introduced an entirely new kind of woman into her mental horizons. Unlike Mrs Austen and so many of their family friends, Eliza seemed free to arrive when she wanted, stay as long as she liked and then disappear again, apparently unencumbered by household management or parental restrictions. In fact, Eliza's life was far from easy, and the distresses over her husband during the French Revolution and her invalid son took their toll. From young Jane's perspective, however, here was a woman who had seen the world, who spoke French as easily as English, who dressed fashionably and brought Parisian manners into rural Hampshire. She was also fond of her English relations, remaining close to Jane and Cassandra as they grew into womanhood and teaching them things that would otherwise have been well outside their experience.

If Eliza was an exciting addition to the circle, however, it was Cassandra who formed its centre, as far as Jane was concerned. Her brothers came and went, creating havoc in their wake, but Cassandra, Jane's only sister, remained a constant, vital source of stability throughout her life. The sisters shared a bedroom, a sense of humour, and a mutual understanding that sustained them both throughout their lives. Though rarely apart even as adults, on occasions when they were staying in different places each wrote frequent letters to the other, as if to deny any thought of separation. From their earliest days, Cassandra was Jane's guide and confidante. As all the family recognised, the girls were everything to each other. It is not surprising, therefore, that when Jane Austen began to write serious novels, the first heroines to appear in her published works were also sisters. Jane's attachment to Cassandra was such that when it was deemed time for Cassandra to receive a more formal education than she was being given at home, Jane was determined to go too. Even though she was only seven, boarding school with Cassandra was better than home without. As her mother commented at the time, 'if Cassandra were going to have her head cut off, Jane would insist on sharing her fate'.[4] In the event, the joke turned rather sour, as both the girls were lucky to survive their school days.

Departure from the family home was not, after all, an exclusively male experience. Jane and Cassandra, together with their cousin Jane Cooper, daughter of Mrs Austen's elder sister, set off for Oxford in the spring of 1783 to be educated by Jane Cooper's aunt, Mrs Cawley, who was the wife of the Principal of Brasenose. The ancient city was also the home of their uncle, Theophilus Leigh, Master of Balliol and subject of endless College anecdotes, and currently of their elder brother, James, who like his father before him, had become a Fellow of St John's. None of this was especially heartening, however, for a seven-year-old girl away from home and surrounded for the first time in her life by the unfamiliar sounds and smells of a city. Mrs Cawley, with her formal manners, would not have seemed much of a substitute for Jane's mother and father, and the exclusive company of little girls could not have been more different from that of the Austen boys. If she had been close to Cassandra before, she now clung to her elder sister for comfort and companionship amidst the 'dismal chapels' and 'dusty libraries'[5] of the medieval seat of learning.

The summer of 1783 was dark and alarming. Gilbert White, who wrote the famous *Natural History* of the Hampshire village of Selborne, recalled the unprecedented heat and humidity, the plagues of wasps and rotting honeysuckle. Even worse were the terrifying meteors and thunderstorms, and the 'smokey fog' that covered the whole of Europe for weeks, 'a most extraordinary appearance, unlike anything known within the memory of man'.[6] We now know that the cause of these startling phenomena was the massive volcanic eruption of Skaptár-jökull in Iceland, but for those witnessing them in England in 1783, the disasters seemed biblical in proportion and mysteriousness. For Jane and Cassandra Austen, the strange summer must have been very frightening indeed, but their fears were compounded by the outbreak of illness at Mrs Cawley's establishment, which led to their removal to Southampton.

The journey from Oxford to the great port on the south coast was slow and tiring, but once in Southampton, well known for its mild air and healthy sea breezes, the girls would be safe. Or this, presumably, was Mrs Cawley's plan. In fact, the city was soon afflicted by an epidemic of typhus fever, which spread alarmingly in the unusually hot summer weather. Despite the danger, Mrs Cawley continued to superintend her charges and decided not to inform their parents, even when both Jane and Cassandra fell seriously ill. It was Jane Cooper who broke the news, and within days of her letter arriving, Mrs Cooper and Mrs Austen were hurrying down to Southampton to collect their children. During the autumn, Jane and Cassandra slowly regained strength at Steventon, but Mrs Cooper, who had also become infected, died.

Despite the experiences of 1783, the Austens decided to send their daughters away again two years later, this time to the Abbey School for Girls in Reading. Although the school was part of a ruined abbey, where ghosts reputedly walked, and where skeletons were certainly uncovered from time to time, the experience seems to have been generally happier than Jane's first foray into formal education. Under the slightly eccentric, but kindly guidance of Mrs Latournelle, with her distinctive cork leg, Jane and Cassandra practised their spelling and handwriting and learned some basic French and Italian, as well as acquiring other specifically female accomplishments, such as needlework and drawing. They also had access to different books in the school library, and very different company in the classroom. Here was an opportunity to make friends independently of her family, and to learn about the various ways in which schoolgirls interact, form close allegiances, compete, console, embrace and exclude one another. Mrs Latournelle's pupils came from other towns and villages, talked of unknown homes and families, and had different ideas about the world and their hopes for the future. Although Jane Austen was only in Reading for two years, and completed her formal schooling by the time she was eleven, her mental field of vision had already widened immeasurably, and her new experiences, deeply mixed as they were, were laid down to ferment in her rich imagination.

Early Writing
1787–92

Although Jane Austen was not at school for very long, her education extended far beyond what was offered by Mrs Cawley and Mrs Latournelle. As Elizabeth Bennet explained to Lady Catherine de Bourgh, even without school or a governess, those who 'wished to learn, never wanted the means'. In *Pride and Prejudice*, Elizabeth's quick wit and elegant choice of words is not attributed to the kind of formal education deemed appropriate for young ladies, but rather to her intellectual freedom – 'We were always encouraged to read.' Once back at home, Jane Austen was similarly at liberty to explore the books owned by her parents and her brothers, and to learn from their wide reading and educated tastes. James, in particular, with his love of poetry and classical literature, helped to encourage his sister's literary knowledge before his marriage to Anne Mathew in 1792. Not only was James eager to discuss literature, he was also keen to write. In addition to composing prologues for the family theatricals, James wrote elegies and sonnets in the style of contemporary poets such as Shenstone and Bowles, and eventually attempted reflective blank verse along the lines of Cowper's new poem, *The Task*. Equally fashionable, if very different in tone, were James's charades, which reflected their mother's comic tastes and aptitude for riddles. When Mr Elton produces his verse puzzle in *Emma*, he is following a model familiar since Jane Austen's childhood.

James's poetry remained unpublished, circulating only among the Austen family. In 1789, however, he launched himself on the public at last, with the help of his younger brother, Henry, in *The Loiterer*. The title was an obvious gesture towards the highly successful literary journals of the day, Dr Johnson's *Idler* or Henry Mackenzie's more recent publication, *The Lounger*. Oxford-based, and Oxford-oriented, *The Loiterer* appeared every Saturday for over a year, offering what the editor promised in the first issue as 'moral lectures, critical remarks, and elegant humour'.

For Jane Austen, now thirteen, the paper also provided a chance for her to see some of her own words in print. In the ninth paper, published 28th March 1789, James included a letter from an unnamed female correspondent, complaining about the male bias of *The Loiterer* and demanding new contributions 'from among the young of both sexes'.[7] Although the authorship of the letter, which was published under the name 'Sophia Sentiment', has never been established absolutely, it seems more than likely that the editor's young sister had a hand in it, and may even have written the entire piece. The playfulness of tone and the parody of sentimental tastes is certainly in accord with Jane Austen's earliest surviving writings, while the comic suggestion for an affecting tale has much in common with the 'Plan for a Novel', which she sent to the Prince Regent's librarian many years later, after the publication of *Emma*: 'let us see some nice affecting stories, relating the misfortunes of two lovers, who died suddenly, just as they were going to church'. The comic conciseness of the sentence, with its abrupt juxtaposition of the clichéd and the unexpected, is as typical of the young Jane Austen as the plot summary that follows: 'Let the lover be killed in a duel, or lost at sea, or you may make him shoot himself, just as you please; and as for his mistress, she will of course go mad; or if you will, you may kill the lady, and let the lover run mad; only remember, whatever you do, that your hero and heroine must possess a good deal of feeling, and have very pretty names.' She may not have written the whole letter, but parts of it seem unmistakably hers.

The letter of Sophia Sentiment is important not only as the first published work of Jane Austen, but also because of its subject matter. Though obviously related to contemporary debates over female education and appropriate reading for girls, Sophia Sentiment (whose name means 'wise opinion' as well as being a parody of the silly fictional heroines of the day) is also a sign of changing attitudes at Steventon. The insertion of a female perspective into the male conversation of *The Loiterer* reveals much about developments within the Austen family in the 1780s, as the younger children began to make their own voices heard. As Jane entered her teens, she was only too conscious of herself as a girl, with feelings and expectations that were very different from most of her siblings. She benefited enormously from the knowledge, advice and encouragement of James and Henry, but obviously recognised that she had her own views, especially when it came to literature. What's more, she was eager to express them.

Jane Austen's early writings were carefully preserved by her family after her death, and so although they were not published until the twentieth century, the three little volumes now provide a rich resource for any reader interested in her work. The pieces she composed between 1787 and 1792 show the early growth of her astonishing literary talent and the way in which it was fostered by her own sense of an immediate audience. Almost every story, poem or playlet is a present to one of her family. 'The Three Sisters' is for 'Edward Austen Esquire', 'The Visit' is dedicated to 'the Revd James Austen', 'The Beautiful Cassandra' to 'Miss Austen', and 'Sir William Mountague' to 'Charles John Austen Esquire'. Some of the creations are offered for a specific purpose, such as 'Frederic and Elfrida' which was given to her close friend, Martha Lloyd, 'As a small testimony of the gratitude I feel for your late generosity to me in finishing my muslin Cloak', or the two little tales, 'Jack and Alice' and

'The Adventures of Mr Harley', which were for Frank, now far away and serving as 'a Midshipman on board his Majesty's ship the Perseverance'.[8] Writing was a way of expressing love and friendship, even if both were apparently being mocked in the stories themselves. 'A Letter from a Young Lady, whose feelings being too Strong for her Judgement led her into the commission of Errors which her Heart disapproved' includes Anna Parker's confession that she murdered her father at a very early period of her life, and has since murdered her mother, before concluding with the resolution, 'I am now going to murder my Sister'. This does not mean that Jane's parents and Cassandra did not enjoy the little spoof just as much as they were meant to. The miniature comedies depend on the improbability of their narratives, and the way in which the familiar is suddenly transformed into something surreal. They also demand an audience who understand the joke.

At every turn, the restrained language of polite eighteenth-century literature is disrupted by unexpected action and often violence. In 'The Beautiful Cassandra', for example, the eponymous heroine falls in love with a particularly pretty bonnet which her mother has been making for the 'Countess of ——'. Taking the bonnet, Cassandra sets off to make her fortune, curtseying to the first young Viscount she meets, before going on towards the bakery. At this point, the comedy explodes:

Chapter the Fourth
She then proceeded to a Pastry-Cooks where she devoured six ices, refused to pay for them, knocked down the Pastry-Cook and walked away.[9]

At twenty-five words, it is not a long chapter, but its effect on the mini-novel is overwhelming. What had begun as a parody of contemporary sentimental fiction suddenly includes a moment of slapstick violence, conveyed with extraordinary verbal economy. The young writer observes the acceptable modes of contemporary writing and behaviour with great astuteness, but is also constantly alert to the possibilities of the unlikely and the unacceptable.

Throughout the early writings, Jane Austen's delight in creating little worlds where anything can happen is abundantly evident. In 'Henry and Eliza', the fairytale detail of the baby discovered in the haycock sets the scene for an extravagant romantic adventure, but its traditional elements are balanced by the distinctive comic outlook that marks so much of Austen's work. When Eliza finds herself imprisoned in Newgate by her persecutor, the Duchess, her response is more reminiscent of Emma Woodhouse than of Cinderella: 'No sooner had Eliza entered her Dungeon than the first thought which occurred to her, was how to get out of it again'.[10] Once she has spent a few weeks working through the bars on her cell window, her escape is hindered by anxiety about her children's safety in the descent down the prison wall. She is, however, a resourceful heroine, and quickly arrives at a solution: 'she determined to fling down all her Clothes, of which she had a large Quantity, and then having given them strict Charge not to hurt themselves, threw her Children after them'. Eliza is both a fairytale character, and a believable young woman in an unbelievable situation.

For despite the wildness of Austen's imaginary incidents, these buoyant stories are generally attached to the ground by numerous details of recognisable human characteristics, turns of phrase or familiar places. Mr Clifford, for example, is introduced through a catalogue of his many carriages ('of which I do not recollect half. I can only remember that he had a Coach, a Chariot, a Chaise, a Landeau, a Landeaulet, a Phaeton, a Gig, a Whisky, an Italian Chair, a Buggy, a Curricle and a wheelbarrow'),[11] but then spends five months laid up in Overton, the town nearest to the Austens' home at Steventon, where he is cured by the celebrated Physician. In other stories, the perspectives of different characters are brilliantly caught, such as that of the postillion, in 'Frederic and Elfrida', whose 'stupidity was amazing', because he declares 'without the least shame or Compunction, that having never been informed he was totally ignorant of what part of the Town, he was to drive to'.[12] The scale and scope of the early pieces may be modest compared with the novels of Austen's maturity, their ambition, however, is anything but. Though the narratives are brief or sometimes seem straining to run away, they are lit by brilliant flashes of observation and by numerous dazzling sentences in which not a word is wasted.

Austen's juvenilia reveal a young writer in the process of self-discovery and a young reader eager to master anything that came her way. She experimented with a remarkable variety of genres, producing playful imitations of contemporary novels, of scenes from Restoration comedy, of comic operettas and conduct manuals, and even composed a short history of England. In every piece, she is in dialogue with established writers, learning from their example, but also daring to take exception to their practices and views, and to put forward her own, highly individual position. The comments she scribbled in Goldsmith's *History of England* reveal a vivid imaginative engagement with his account of the English past, as she laments the fate of Christopher Layer, hung, drawn and quartered for his support of Ormond: 'Poor Man! Alas Poor Man', or responds to the detail of Cromwell's massacre of Drogheda, 'Detestable Monster!'.[13] Imaginative reading was the prelude to imaginative writing, and when Jane Austen turned her hand to British history, her own account was just as full of sympathetic involvement with figures such as Elizabeth Woodville, 'who, poor Woman!, was afterwards confined in a Convent by that Monster of Iniquity and Avarice Henry the 7th'.[14]

Everything she read came alive, but at the same time, her natural empathy with those she encountered through her reading was kept in check by a keen sense of the ridiculous and of the potential absurdity of emotional display. When Charlotte reflects on the unfortunate predicament of her double engagement in

'Jack and Alice', for example, her suicidal plunge is treated with high good humour: 'She floated to Crankhumdunberry where she was picked up and buried.' Austen even composes a comic epitaph in the manner of contemporary commemorative tablets:

Here lies our friend who having promis-ed
That unto two she would be marri-ed
Threw her sweet Body and her lovely face
Into the Stream that runs thro' Portland Place.

Austen's love of literary form and her delight in the comic potential of language would always prevent her sympathetic nature from emanating in sentimentality on the page. The girl who chose to give her pastoral heroine, Chloe, a song in which she yearns for Strephon to carve the partridge 'if it should be a tough one, Tough one, tough one, tough one'[15] would never allow her pen to dwell in the regions of simple romance. When Jane Austen presented Jane Cooper with an elaborately allitera-tive dedication, she signed herself 'your Comical Cousin'. In her early writings, she was not only developing her literary skills, but also learning to define herself.

As a young writer, Jane Austen wanted to find out what she could do. As one of the youngest in a large family, she also wanted to show everyone else what she had found. Making people laugh was also a way of making them listen. For although her miniature novels were often written for her closest companion and most sympathetic reader, Cassandra, much of her early writing seems designed to impress as well as to entertain. One of the most substantial pieces, which must have demanded considerable authorial effort, is 'Love and Freindship', dedicated to Jane's sophisticated older cousin, Eliza. As if to bridge the age difference between the young author and her patroness, now turning thirty, the little epistolary tale begins as the heroine reaches fifty-five, and is assumed by her younger correspondent to be safe at last 'from the determined Perseverance of disagreeable Lovers and the cruel Persecutions of obstinate Fathers'. Fifty-five-year-old Laura is less convinced that the time for adventures is over, but nevertheless agrees to unfold the story of her life so far, in a series of letters that effectively parody every cliché of the contemporary literature of sensibility.

Some of the earliest pieces were for Jane's parents. In 'The Mystery', she humbly solicits the patronage of her father, in a dedication which is parodic, but still expresses a child's desire for parental approval. As the youngest daughter, Jane probably had to work quite hard to attract attention from her busy parents, and so her talent for creating amusing stories was a very happy discovery. Though younger than her brothers, and educated according to the expectations of an age in which women of her class were expected to marry and have babies rather than to pursue an academic education or a profession, Jane Austen's natural ability and determination enabled her to excel her literary siblings from a very early age. To the great credit of her parents, they encouraged rather than curbed her genius, and so the dedications of her early compositions convey a genuine debt of gratitude as well as mockery of contemporary literary fashions.

Despite Jane Austen's early discovery of the possibilities of the page, her writings also reveal an awareness of potential limitation. The earliest surviving pieces offer not only playful miniaturisation of contemporary literary styles, but also an acute sense of the prospects open to young women. 'Amelia Webster', a diminutive example of the epistolary fiction popular in Austen's childhood, manages to introduce three different couples and conclude with their marriages in the space of seven very short letters between the various characters and the unknown observers, Tom and Jack. 'Edgar and Emma', a slightly more substantial narrative in the third person, depicts the return of Sir Godfrey and Lady Marlow to their family seat after an absence of two years, and its profound effect on their daughter, Emma, who has been nursing a passion for Edgar Willmot.

Emma's discovery that of all the numerous Willmot children (the list runs to more than twenty), Edgar is away at college, produces a powerful reaction: 'she remained however tolerably composed till the Willmot's were gone when having no check to the overflowings of her grief, she gave free vent to them, and retiring to her own room, continued in tears the remainder of her Life'. Although the comic excesses of the tale are beautifully handled, it offers an alternative ending to the happy unions that so quickly bring closure to 'Amelia Webster'. Even at the age of twelve, Jane Austen was aware that there seemed only two possible endings for a young woman's story – either marriage or melancholy isolation. Her tales show not only her early, assured sense of the way narrative works, but also an understanding of the limited choices open to young women, whatever their natural ability.

By 1792, the comic energy of her tales was as vigorous as ever, but they also reveal a growing interest in human situations and prospects. In 'Catharine', for example, the sentimental heroine's refuge in her favourite bower provides the centrepiece for parodying contemporary literary convention, but it also offers a space for more serious reflection on the fate of those who had helped create the shady arbour – the Wynne sisters. Catharine's close friends had lost their parents, and therefore their home and financial security; as a result, one was now 'Splendidly, yet unhappily married' while the other, 'scarcely more comfortable', had been employed as a companion to the daughters of a dowager.[16] The story begins by reducing two young women to lives of misery, which leaves the bereft Catharine to an uncertain future at the mercy of her aunt and neighbours. The author's acute awareness of the precariousness of human life and especially of young women's fortunes gives the unfinished tale an edge that is quite different from the extravagant freedom of some of the earlier pieces. At sixteen, she was alert not only to the ways in which fictional narrative worked, but also to the less manageable stories of real men and women.

As her elder brothers, Edward and James, married and set up homes of their own, the pressure to find a suitable partner was beginning to bear upon the younger members of the household. While Jane Austen was imagining the future of Catharine in her bower, her cousin, Jane Cooper, was being swept away in a whirlwind romance and marriage to a handsome Captain in the Navy. When Revolutionary France declared war the following February, Henry enlisted at once in the Oxfordshire Militia. Charles was already at the Royal Naval Academy at Portsmouth and would soon follow Frank into active service at sea. For Jane Austen at seventeen, the prospect of eventually being left alone in a large house with aging parents was just beginning to seem threatening to a degree that could not be entirely dispelled.

The True Art of Letter-Writing
1793–7

When Catherine Morland tells Mr Tilney that 'one day in the country is exactly like another', she is reflecting the experience of a young woman whose life until the age of seventeen has been spent in 'a small retired village', and who now finds herself amid the bustle and variety of Bath. In 1797, at the age of twenty-one, Jane Austen visited the fashionable spa town for the first time, and the fear and excitement of being jostled in the crowded Assembly Rooms and thronging streets went straight into the novel she began to write on her return to Steventon. Unlike Catherine, however, Jane Austen had already realised that Bath's attractions, considerable as they were, could not necessarily eclipse the appeal of rural life. Tiny villages and elegant towns both had their merits, however different in kind. What *Northanger Abbey* demonstrates is that by the end of the 1790s, Jane Austen was in a position to recreate either within the pages of a novel, and to develop fictional voices capable of presenting opposing points of view with complete conviction. The difference between her work at the beginning and end of the decade is remarkable, and even though nothing she completed at this period was published within her lifetime, it represents a crucial stage of Jane Austen's development, both as a writer and as a woman.

Although Catherine Morland might not have noticed much going on before her arrival in Bath, life at Steventon was full of drama. If the outbreak of war turned Henry into a tall, scarlet-coated lieutenant, it also placed him in potentially mortal danger, deepened by his own determination to obtain a commission in the regular army rather than the militia. Even in the militia, he was rapidly sent off to Southampton to defend the realm against the very real threat of a French invasion. Hampshire, a county on the south coast of England, whose harbours accommodated the principal naval ports of Portsmouth and Southampton, was in the front line of any imminent attack: if the Revolutionary forces were victorious, the area around Steventon would be one of the first to fall into enemy hands. Nor were the fears merely generated by newspaper reports of distant political developments. In the summer of 1794, Jane's cousin Eliza returned to the Rectory, traumatised by her experiences in France, and full of overwhelming memories of what she had witnessed. She had reached Calais, heavily pregnant, given birth to a baby who died almost at once, and then escaped across the Channel. On top of the distress and physical upheaval, she had to contend with the thoughts of her husband's trial, the hostile evidence of their own servants, and his death on the guillotine. Eliza had grown up in India and travelled across half the world, but nothing had prepared her for the shock of a familiar European country convulsed in revolution.

If Eliza's experiences in the 1790s were bound up with the great historic events of the period, other members of Jane Austen's family were experiencing things that might not register publicly but were just as momentous personally. The marriages of Edward and James were followed a year later by the births of their children Fanny and Anna, giving Jane and Cassandra new identities in the family – as aunts. James and his wife moved with the new baby into the rectory at Deane, within a mile of Steventon, where James had become the curate and worked under his father's guidance. Little Anna would never remember her mother, however, for James's wife, Anne, died suddenly in May 1795. Within two years he had married again, choosing for his bride Mary Lloyd, who was not to prove the easiest stepmother for his daughter, though she swiftly provided a son and heir to carry James's name and genes into the next generation. As James planned his second wedding, Eliza was also ready to exchange widowhood for marriage to her long-standing admirer, Henry Austen, now old enough to seem a suitable partner and full of just the kind of optimistic energy to help renew her hopes and happiness.

Cassandra, too, seemed destined to escape her role as sister, daughter and aunt, for she had become engaged to Thomas Fowle, former student at the Rectory, now ordained as a clergyman and hoping to establish himself in a satisfactory living. If Jane's delight in her sister's happiness was tinged with some private dismay at the thought of their permanent separation, she was still quick to sympathise with Cassandra when it emerged that instead of an early wedding, Tom Fowle would be disappearing overseas for many months. When asked to accompany his uncle, Lord Craven, across the Atlantic as the chaplain on board his boat, Tom agreed to go. With Frank and Charles already in the Navy, the Austens knew all about the hazards and discomfort of long voyages and were only too aware of the likelihood of a hostile confrontation with the enemy fleet. In the event, Tom suffered not from the French, but from a fever, dying in St Domingo in 1798 before he and Cassandra had a chance to marry.

Upheavals such as these at home and abroad must have had their effects on all concerned. And what was Jane Austen doing during the tumultuous 1790s? She seems to have spent most of her time dancing. 'I fancy I could just as well dance for a week together as for half an hour', she wrote on Christmas Eve, 1798, capturing the mood of the night before and of much of the preceding decade. It is not until January 1796 that modern readers get a proper glimpse of the young Jane Austen, speaking in her own voice to the person closest to her. Her earliest surviving letter to Cassandra was written over a January weekend, when Jane was twenty and her elder sister was celebrating her twenty-third birthday with her fiancé, whose family lived in Kintbury, not far from the market town of Newbury. Her birthday greeting is just as light-hearted as the compositions she had given Cassandra in the past, hoping that her sister 'will live twenty three years longer', before moving swiftly on to the real present – an account of last night's ball. After giving details of various members of the party, she admits, teasingly, 'I am almost afraid to tell you how my Irish friend and I behaved.' The details are withheld with just the same control that she would later exert on the narration of her novels, and just the same encouragement to let the mind race on: 'Imagine to yourself everything most profligate and shocking in the way of dancing and sitting down together.' Whatever the pleasures of Kintbury, some part of Cassandra must have been eager to know more about her sister's evening with Jane's 'Irish friend', Tom Lefroy.

Jane's Tom lived in Ireland, but had spent Christmas visiting his relatives at Ashe, a village close to Steventon and Deane. Jane was especially fond of Mrs Lefroy, and so she found herself attending the same balls as Mrs Lefroy's nephew and evidently enjoying his company very much, despite meeting him on only three occasions. Though apparently sanguine about his imminent departure (which would leave 'nothing to console us till the arrival of the Coopers on Tuesday'), she describes him as 'a very gentlemanlike, good-looking, pleasant young man', and towards the end of the letter admits that he had 'but *one* fault... that his morning coat is a great deal too light'. The detail is really an excuse to compare Tom Lefroy to Fielding's impulsive and hugely attractive hero, Tom Jones, and to convey to Cassandra that their profligate and shocking conversations had involved discussion of a decidedly risqué novel.

Five days later, she wrote again to mark the day 'on which I am to flirt my last with Tom Lefroy', adding 'My tears flow as I write, at the melancholy idea.' Her language recalls the sentimental heroines of her early parodies, and shows that her command of exaggerated emotional expression could be usefully applied in the management of her own feelings. If Cassandra doubted her tone for a moment, she would have been reassured by the very next sentence, which announces that William Chute had called the day before, and includes a typical comic touch: 'I wonder what he means by being so civil.' It is hardly the letter of a broken-hearted damsel, but it does convey very powerfully the sense of a young woman enjoying life, discovering her own sexual feelings and recognising that she herself was poised for adventures in the adult world.

Throughout her twenties, Jane Austen's letters are filled with news of balls and ball-gowns. Though she wrote to Cassandra only when they were apart and some of the correspondence was destroyed, the surviving letters give a vivid sense of Jane Austen's life and opinions as a young woman. The 'true art of letter-writing', she observed on 3rd January 1801, was 'to express on paper exactly what one would say to the same person by word of mouth'. Reading her letters to Cassandra thus gives us the privileged sense of eavesdropping on their conversations. Their close relationship meant that Jane could express her feelings freely, in terms that she knew would be understood and received with kindness. After a Christmas Ball in 1798 she was riding on a cloud of warm memories, after dancing all twenty dances – 'My black Cap was openly admired by Mrs Lefroy, & secretly I imagine by every body else in the room', but a fortnight later, things turned out rather less happily – 'I do not think I was very much in request – People were rather apt not to ask me till they could not help it.' Personal disappointments nevertheless afforded comic opportunities, and so the very good looking officer who had apparently been so keen to meet her is despatched in her letter with easy wit – 'as he did not want it quite enough to take much trouble in effecting it, We never could bring it about'. The voice is irrepressibly lively even in the most challenging of social minefields. If she was disappointed by Tom Lefroy's failure to visit her when he stayed with his aunt in November 1798 some three years after their flirtation, the letter which refers to the discovery betrays little visible sign of distress, and carries on with typical witty observations on Mary (who would be 'glad to get rid of' her rheumatism, and her child) and Mrs Portman ('not much admired in Dorsetshire; the good-natured world, as usual, extolled her beauty so highly, that all the neighbourhood have had the pleasure of being disappointed'). It is not that Jane Austen lacked deep feeling, but her favourite mode for letters, as for every other kind of writing, was comic.

Although it is possible to detect in her private correspondence some of the emotional upheavals experienced during the 1790s, the surviving letters also bubble with excitement over new experiences, revelations about human nature, flirtatious conversations and hopes of even better encounters to come. They suggest a young woman who is keen to share her experiences and observations, but who is always writing primarily to entertain an affectionate reader. When she arrived in London in August 1796, for example, she reached at once for pen and paper, adopting a familiar parodic tone to convey her obvious relish of the great city: 'Here I am once more in this Scene of Dissipation & vice, and I begin already to find my Morals corrupted.' Three years later, when she travelled to Bath, the same air of excitement runs through the account sent to Cassandra, but this time there are more witty comments on those she had encountered, like 'Dr Hall in such deep mourning that either his Mother, his Wife, or Himself must be dead'. The apparent suppression of sympathy in observations of this kind is really an expression of feeling for someone who mattered more to her than Dr Hall, and who would recognise the tone of the sentence instantly. Jane Austen's references to death and disease were very often pithily phrased, as if to emphasise the comic absurdity of the human condition when its most vulnerable aspects were being exposed.

She wanted to make Cassandra laugh – just as Cassandra's letters had pleased her. We no longer have the letters sent by Cassandra, but numerous references in Jane's correspondence suggest that they were a source of great enjoyment – 'The letter which I have this moment received from you has diverted me beyond moderation', she wrote on 1st September, 1796, 'I could die of laughter at it, as they used to say at school.' Cassandra's fine letters set high standards, and Jane replies by calling her 'the finest comic writer of the present age', a compliment reminiscent of the extravagant dedications in her early writings, but also indicative of Jane's own values and aims.

Occasionally, the letters do reveal her anxieties, as in the one despatched on 18th September 1796, from Edward's home at Rowling in Kent, which begins with a confession that the morning has been spent 'in Doubt and Deliberation', and ends with a rare, but telling apology: 'How ill I have written. I begin to hate myself.' Throughout the letter, Jane Austen's uncertainty about how she was going to get home to Steventon undermines her determined comedy, and gives her joke about falling into the hands of 'some fat Woman who would make me drunk with Small Beer' an uncomfortable edge. Letters such as this afford a sharp insight into Jane Austen's utter dependency on her relations and her own fundamental lack of freedom. Generally, her writing offered a world in which she was in command, but here the pressures of a situation which rendered her powerless to make decisions was disrupting the smooth control of her prose.

Although Jane Austen spent so much of her young adulthood planning her wardrobe and enjoying parties, writing remained crucial to her sense of self and general wellbeing. Her first surviving novel demonstrates the care that she devoted to her creative work during the 1790s, and the continuing force of her experimental spirit. 'Lady Susan' is a remarkable transitional text, retaining all the irreverence of her earliest work, but revealing as well many of the strengths of her maturity. It is designed to startle readers – and a glance through the responses it has elicited over the years shows that it has been very successful in this respect. Though epistolary in form, the fictional letters in 'Lady Susan' are most unlike those written by Jane to Cassandra, since they are used to construct distinct characters, who are often motivated by a self-seeking desire to influence their correspondents. When inviting herself to her brother-in-law's house at the start of the novel, for example, Lady Susan is a model of politeness and propriety, but to her admirer, Reginald, she presents the tones of passionate indignation. Only Mrs Johnson is allowed to read about her friend Lady Susan's calculated manipulation of all those she encounters, and even these letters seem chiefly designed to show off secret triumphs to a less successful woman of the world.

The discrepancy between Lady Susan's fond references to her daughter in the opening letter to Mr Vernon and the subsequent assessment sent to Mrs Johnson – 'She is a stupid girl, & has nothing to recommend her'[17] – could hardly be more marked. Jane Austen is revelling in the possibilities of skilled language, and discovering that words are as prone to deceive as to reveal the truth. Lady Susan is a brilliant writer, who knows the power of a good narrative – 'I trust I shall be able to make my story as good as her's. If I am vain of anything, it is of my eloquence.' Though she has struck many readers as a monster of amorality, she is also in part a fantasy figure for a young woman whose own life offered so few real choices, and whose chance for personal autonomy depended on her imagination and skills as a writer. Lady Susan's 'desire for dominion' and love of 'universal admiration' may be despised by her sister-in-law, Mrs Vernon, but they reflect something of the author behind the fiction, who seems to have used her novel to start exploring some of the complexities of the human psyche and of the relations between different people. A woman who, despite her fading beauty, could command the desire of every man she encountered and whose primary means to control her world were linguistic, had an attraction that extended beyond the eyes of her fictional suitors. At the same time, the abhorrence of Lady Susan that is manifest in so many of the letters suggests an acute awareness of the potentially unappealing nature of eloquence and of the dislike so easily generated by an intelligent woman who might be deemed cunning, unmaternal or coquettish. Lady Susan is at once attractive and repulsive, and the choice of the letter form allows conflicting responses to exist side by side.

The satirical comedy of 'Lady Susan' seems less exaggerated than that of Austen's earlier writing because the characters are more developed and the situations more realistic, but the novel is still full of similar jokes. Lady Susan's dismay at being forced to visit 'that insupportable Spot, a country village' is clearly meant to amuse the Austen family, as is her observation that 'I have never yet found that the advice of a Sister could prevent a young Man's being in love if he chose it.' It is also easy to hear Jane Austen's enjoyment of verbal economy in Lady Susan's advice to Mrs Johnson on the management of husbands: 'since he will be stubborn, he must be tricked'. Integral to the humour, however, is a more serious concern with human behaviour and social codes. The novel gave Jane Austen an opportunity to air some of her exasperation with contemporary notions about the education of girls, as Lady Susan despatches her daughter to a fashionable boarding school, despite believing that being 'Mistress of French, Italian, German, Music, Singing, Drawing &c will gain a Woman some applause, but will not add one Lover to her list'. Frederica's desperate escape from the school and the subsequent revelation of her fondness for independent reading is more than a joke at her mother's expense, and conveys Jane Austen's own dissatisfaction with the way in which so many girls seemed born only to be groomed for the marriage market and dissuaded from taking independent action by domineering adults who rendered them virtual prisoners in their own families. Frederica's story is in some ways a comical revisiting of the great epistolary novels of Samuel Richardson, but it also hints that the parodic surface of Jane Austen's early fiction was beginning to reveal new depths of sympathy and engagement with the predicaments of real people.

The sympathy for Frederica that increasingly undermines Lady Susan's domination of her novel is a good indication of

Jane Austen's literary development. Despite her attraction to the comic potential of the older woman in fiction, Austen herself was only just entering her twenties and her imagination was more readily engaged by the possibilities and difficulties facing those of her own age. From Lady Susan, she turned her attentions to new, younger characters in the creation of two novels that would eventually be revised and published as *Sense and Sensibility* and *Pride and Prejudice*. Unfortunately, the manuscripts of the works composed in the 1790s have not been preserved, so we can only speculate on the shape of 'Elinor and Marianne' and 'First Impressions'. It seems likely that both were at least partially epistolary in form like 'Lady Susan', and that some of the letters included in *Sense and Sensibility* and *Pride and Prejudice* had their origins in Jane Austen's earlier compositions. The focus of the later plots on young women in search of suitable partners, who suffer setbacks from unreliable men, overbearing relations and social prejudices, also has obvious foundations in the kind of life led by their author during the 1790s. More than this, however, can hardly be ascertained with any confidence.

What is clear, nevertheless, is that Jane's writing continued to command the respect of her family. An anecdote in her niece Anna Lefroy's 'Recollections' describes an early family reading of *Pride and Prejudice*, which was thought unsuitable for the ears of such a little girl, but still shows how much her older relations enjoyed Aunt Jane's stories.[18] For her nineteenth birthday, George Austen made a symbolic gesture of support by presenting Jane with a writing desk, but by November 1797, he was ready to make the more public statement of offering his daughter's novel to the leading London publishing house of Cadell and Davies. 'First Impressions' was back by return of post, but the very possibility of publication was a major step. It seemed only a matter of time before the talented young woman would turn into a published author.

Bath
1798–1804

'Well here we are at Bath.' When Jane Austen wrote to Cassandra in May 1799, at the beginning of a six-week visit, she was in good spirits, despite the dismal weather and her mother's ill health. As she had been to Bath before, her references to the fashionable venues and elegant streets – Sydney Gardens, Paragon, Queen's Parade – have the ease of familiarity as well as the frisson of expectation. In the weeks that followed, she became more optimistic about her mother's recovering strength and felt free to fill Cassandra in on the latest fashions in headwear and the most recent additions to their social circle. Eighteen months later, her attitude to Bath had changed completely. Instead of inhabiting her imagination as a dazzling white city, full of exciting strangers and outlandish outfits, offering the endless diversions of theatres, shops and public assemblies, it had become the destination of a dwindling family who were leaving their home for ever.

In 1800, George Austen announced his plan to retire from his duties as the parish priest in Steventon and to settle in Bath. Jane, as an unmarried daughter, would of course accompany her parents, and so by New Year, she was planning her departure from the house where she had been born and lived for twenty-five years. Family recollections have led to a general perception that the removal from beloved Hampshire to Bath was one of the great disasters of Jane Austen's life, but there is, as so often, very little direct evidence of her feelings on the matter. The letter she wrote in January 1801 is full of practical details about the relative living costs of different parts of Bath, but says little about her attachment to Steventon. Nevertheless, her confession to Cassandra, 'I get more & more reconciled to the idea of our removal', suggests that the prospect of dislocation had been decidedly unwelcome. Nor is this very surprising, for an exceptionally sensitive woman whose entire life had centred on a country rectory surrounded by beautiful, rolling hills, thick with every kind of tree and crossed by lanes whose secrets seemed to be held by the high hedges that arched above. Bath had its own beauty. It was an exciting place to visit. But the idea of living there permanently was a very different matter.

Jane's explanation to Cassandra of her gradual reconciliation to the departure plan suggests a determination to find some positive angle on a catastrophe: 'We have lived long enough in this Neighbourhood, the Basingstoke Balls are certainly on the decline, there is something in the bustle of going away, & the prospect of spending future summers by the Sea or in Wales is very delightful.' The rapid accumulation of arguments makes each seem less persuasive than the one before. Just as Elinor Dashwood would counsel her devastated younger sister to exert herself and conceal her distresses, Jane Austen appears to be rallying her own powers of self-possession in order to face an unavoidable fact. As her letter continues, she claims that leaving Steventon is no great sacrifice, and that she expects 'to inspire no tenderness, no interest in those we leave behind'. She is effectively voicing the lesson later inflicted on Anne Elliot at her most self-punishing, 'in the art of knowing our own nothingness beyond our own circle'.

Whatever the degree of distress induced by the departure from Hampshire, however, Bath did offer the possibility of a new life. Living in town might be noisy and unsettling, but it also meant a lot more people, some of whom might eventually emerge from the crowd as friends or even prospective husbands. As Jane Austen entered her late twenties, the pressure to marry was becoming more intense, so perhaps the balls in Bath would produce the right man at last? Any lingering thoughts about Tom Lefroy's admiration had taken on a very different complexion when the news of his marriage to the Irish heiress, Mary Paul, had arrived in 1799. The other men who figured in her letters had either found new girls to dance with, or moved away, or simply failed to ignite any real passion in her heart. Surely there was someone in Bath? And even if both she and Cassandra were destined to remain single, the complete change of scenery, of daily routines and activities, would surely provide an immense boost to her writing.

When she first returned from the city in 1797, her imagination had, after all, been fired by a new sense of possibility. The reaction to a first encounter with Bath recorded in *Northanger Abbey* is drawn straight from recent experience – 'They arrived at Bath. Catherine was all eager delight; – her eyes were here, there, every where, as they approached its fine and striking environs, and afterwards drove through those streets which conducted them to the hotel. She was come to be happy, and she felt happy already.' Thoughts of Bath could generate intense happiness, and Jane Austen knew that very well. But the pleasures of life in the city could also seem superficial and artificial, just like its residents. By the time she was revising the novel for publication during 1801 and 1802, her own ideas about Bath had undergone very substantial alteration.

Although no manuscript has survived to offer clues about which passages belong to particular periods of composition, it seems likely that those conveying some of the less positive aspects of Bath belong to the process of revision rather than to the initial burst of creativity. In a conversation over the attractions of Bath, the newcomer's keen appetite for everything the city has to offer is carefully balanced against the more jaded perspective of the habitual visitor. Catherine's eager exclamations, 'Oh! Who can ever be tired of Bath?' are carefully juxtaposed with Mr Tilney's more considered assessment, 'For six weeks I allow, Bath is pleasant enough; but beyond *that*, it is the most tiresome place in the world.' Neither view is complete, but together they may reflect Jane Austen's growing ability to invest traditional literary themes with the freshness of first-hand observation. In the same decade that William Blake created his *Songs of Innocence* and *Experience*, Jane Austen was exploring the contrary states in relation to her own life and her literary development.

If, during her teens, Jane Austen had considered herself like Catherine Morland, as being 'in training for a heroine', it was now perhaps dawning on her that she was more suited to take on the role of author. The narrative voice in *Northanger Abbey*, though infinitely sympathetic, is keen to emphasise the distance between the perspective of the story-teller and that of the main character. The rapid summary of Catherine Morland's life prior to seventeen introduces readers to the affectionate irony of the all-seeing narrator, but offers no direct communication from the heroine herself. We do not hear Catherine's voice properly until half way through the second chapter, when she whispers to Mrs Allen in the packed Upper Rooms, 'How uncomfortable it is not to have a single acquaintance here.' The difference between the heroine's own words and the highly sophisticated sentences that have prepared the way for her debut is only too apparent, and while the novel steadily allows for increasing focus on Catherine's interior drama, its interest is sustained throughout by the narrator's self-consciously skilful commentary.

The joke about Catherine's status as a heroine is a natural development from the parodic character of Jane Austen's early writings. Her teenage compositions reveal a fascination with literary convention which continues to emerge in *Northanger Abbey*. The novel is much more substantial than early pieces such as 'The Beautiful Cassandra' or 'Henry and Eliza', with the exploration of literary matters integrated into a narrative that offers the additional satisfactions of convincing settings, astute observation, imaginative involvement with the characters and a proper plot. Its author had learned much about the development of different characters and the ways in which contrasting ideas could be conveyed through their letters when she wrote *Lady Susan*, but these discoveries were only the forerunners of what she achieved in *Northanger Abbey*. One of the most obvious differences between the two works is that of form. As Mrs Morland says goodbye to her daughter at the beginning of *Northanger Abbey*, the narrator observes that 'It is remarkable... that she neither insisted on Catherine's writing by every post, nor exacted her promise of transmitting the character of every new acquaintance, nor a detail of every interesting conversation that Bath might produce.' In effect, Jane Austen was despatching her heroine on her adventures and the epistolary novel to the honourable shades of literary history. Once she had abandoned the letter form favoured by Samuel Richardson and Frances Burney for their highly influential novels about the social challenges facing young women in the eighteenth century, Jane Austen was free to develop her own, independent narrative voice. Though she did not realise it at the time, she was also pioneering an entirely new kind of English fiction.

Jane Austen could not have predicted the future of the English novel when she worked on *Northanger Abbey*, but she was certainly very conscious of the possibilities of her chosen form. She also knew that not everyone was as enlightened. Before the family moved from Steventon, a circulating library had opened in the village, which allowed local people to borrow books and thus greatly increase their scope for reading. When the proprietor asked the Austens to subscribe in December 1798, she assured them that her library would stock not just novels, but all kinds of literature, an overture which produced some amusement at the Rectory: 'She might have spared this pretension to *our* family, who are great Novel-readers & not ashamed of being so' though they recognised that Mrs Martin's reassurances were probably necessary 'to the self-consequence of half of her Subscribers'. Today, the genre is so well established that it is hard to imagine a time when people were embarrassed to admit to being 'Novel-readers', but when Jane Austen was alive, novels were widely regarded as somewhat frivolous and even downright dangerous. For girls, especially, reading fiction was often considered risky and generally undesirable. It was not every clergyman who would choose the latest Gothic fiction for his holiday reading, but Jane Austen describes her father engrossed in *The Midnight Bell* at the 'Bull and George' in Dartford, on their way home from Kent in October 1798. Even more unusual, though, was George Austen's readiness to share such books with his unmarried daughters.

When Jane Austen depicted Catherine Morland being introduced to the newest 'Horrid Novels' by Isabella Thorpe, she was playing on contemporary fears about the harmful influence of fiction, but with characteristic refusal to submit to prevailing assumptions, she used the scene as an opportunity to defend her favourite literary form. In answer to the dismissive attitude so common among her contemporaries – 'Oh! It is only a novel!' – the narrator of *Northanger Abbey* famously retorts, 'only some work in which the greatest powers of the mind are displayed, in which the most thorough knowledge of human nature, the happiest delineation of its varieties, the liveliest effusions of wit and humour are conveyed to the world in the best chosen language'. As she worked on her own novel, Jane Austen was beginning to recognise just what a task she was undertaking.

The celebration of fiction in *Northanger Abbey* extends well beyond the startling defence in chapter five. John Thorpe's failure to get through more than the first volume of Frances Burney's new novel is an indication of his other deficiencies, while Henry Tilney's detailed knowledge of Mrs Radcliffe's work is one of his many charms. Although Catherine herself is led into excruciating misunderstandings by her undisciplined, Gothic-fuelled imagination, her unaffected pleasure in books, as in everything else, delights all those she meets, especially her own readers. As Jane Austen presented her heroine interpreting her life according to the books she has enjoyed, she was exploring the complexities of her own art and her responsibilities as a writer. When Catherine exclaims at Northanger, 'Oh! Mr Tilney, how frightful! – This is just like a book!', she demonstrates her author's sophisticated understanding of the dimensions of fiction. Not only does the narrator prompt us to consider what we are doing when we read a novel, but so do the characters. Catherine Morland's propensity to see herself in a fictional world is, after all, understandable enough, given that she is a character in a novel.

In her early writing, Jane Austen had moved happily between the recognisable world of Hampshire and the realms of her own reading, revelling in the comedy that could be extracted from sudden jumps from one to another. Now she explored an altogether more subtle kind of fiction, in which the literary and the real cohabited far more harmoniously. Crucial to the success of her new novel was its more realistic representation of settings, conversations and action. Familiarity with Bath enabled Jane Austen to create a fictional world that instantly rings true. Unlike the Scottish or Welsh references in 'Lesley Castle' or 'Love and Freindship', the city in *Northanger Abbey* is a real place, conjured up by the names of streets and buildings that occur naturally in the course of the narrative. 'They were soon settled in comfortable lodgings in Pulteney-Street' has a matter-of-fact quality that enables readers to enter into the world of the novel, whether or not they have any first-hand knowledge of Bath. The description of Catherine's journey through Laura-Place and into Argyle Buildings in John Thorpe's carriage is so convincing that the heroine's distress seems only too real, just as her subsequent enjoyment of the ball is enhanced for readers by its taking place in the Octagon Room. No detailed description of the architecture of Bath is offered, but the way in which both characters and narrator refer to the various venues, just as readers might describe things to a local friend, is far more effective than an elaboration of sash windows, Sheraton tables and chandeliers.

Bath offered more than a rich landscape for Jane Austen's characters, however. Apart from her early educational experiences, Jane Austen had spent much of her life in the company of her own extended family and with those who lived in the parsonages and manor houses round about. She knew the servants at home, and the labourers who worked in the nearby fields. She went to the shops in Overton and to balls in Basingstoke. She had stayed in Kent when visiting Edward's family and had been to London to see Henry. Apart from this, however, her experience of human life was not very extensive, and so Bath's appeal to people of all ages and very varied backgrounds greatly increased her knowledge of the world. Mrs Allen's obsession with muslins, for example, is beautifully observed, and though reminiscent in some ways of Charlotte Luttrell's preoccupation with food in 'Lesley Castle', conveys all the atmosphere of 1790s Bath. Nor was it just the enormous range of individuals who came and went for their health or for the social season. Jane Austen was able to experience life in town, and to develop ways of recreating a smart, urban environment in her fiction. Catherine Morland's first excursion vividly evokes the alarm that may be felt by a girl from the country who finds herself overwhelmed by a mass of strangers in a confined space. Once adjusted to Bath, however, Catherine is able to navigate the streets with ease, while her creator uses the skilfully evoked sense of endless movement to introduce new characters and chance encounters unexpectedly, and yet not improbably.

If Bath provided a stimulating environment for Jane Austen's active imagination, it also offered daily reminders of what might result from her determined efforts to find the best language for her wit and humour. In Steventon, the opening of a circulating library was a major event. Bath, on the other hand, was so well endowed with bookshops and libraries that the Austen family were able to keep up with the latest publications far more easily. To be surrounded by new books and, equally important, by the people who bought new books, was probably as important to

Jane Austen's development as the fresh material that furnished her inner world. Although 'First Impressions' had been rejected out of hand, it seemed worth having another attempt at convincing a publisher that her work was worth his attention. Crosby and Co had outlets in the Bath book trade and published a considerable range of titles, including domestic and Gothic novels. The firm was doing well, made efforts to market its books effectively and welcomed 'eye-catching' scripts.[19] Henry was now established as a banker in London, and with the help of one of his new contacts, William Seymour, Jane Austen's novel found its way into the offices of Crosby and Co early in 1803. To the author's very great delight, it was accepted.

At this stage of its development, the novel eventually published as *Northanger Abbey* was called 'Susan', a title that made its first public appearance within months of the publisher's acceptance, among the lists of new books being advertised by Crosby. Such rapid literary success must have done much to ease any residual sadness over the departure from rural Hampshire, and helped with the reconciliation to the Austens' new urban lifestyle. Not yet thirty, Jane Austen's talents were being recognised beyond the warm but inevitably partial gaze of her immediate family. The ability that had always been channelled into private entertainments was now to find a much larger audience. 'Susan' was about to make her entrance into society, and was ready to be jostled and admired by a crowd of unknown readers.

The novel, however, did not appear. Despite his agreement to publish, and the fee of £10 that Crosby sent in return for the manuscript, his firm never printed 'Susan'. Nor did he give any reason for his decision to withhold publication. Gradually, the months of waiting for news of the book turned into years. The heady joy of being accepted became the hard fact of being rejected. For a single woman approaching her thirtieth birthday in the early nineteenth century, the feeling of being unwanted was beginning to close in from various directions.

From Home to Home
1804—9

'But you know we must marry.'[20] It is not difficult to discern some of Jane Austen's own preoccupations behind the dialogue she began to draft after her first novel had been sent off to the publishers. She abandoned 'The Watsons' after only forty pages, but what survives of her new story reveals much about a writer whose life seemed oddly suspended between hope and disappointment. The fragment opens with Emma Watson returning to her real family after growing up in the happy home of an aunt who had just remarried and gone to join her new husband in Ireland. On the journey into Surrey, Emma is accompanied by her elder sister, Elizabeth, who seizes the opportunity to recount the sorry tale of her broken romance, while insisting that she must nevertheless find a husband. The reason why the Watson sisters are faced with no alternative to an early marriage is economic: 'Father cannot provide for us, & it is very bad to grow old & be poor & laughed at.' Emma is nevertheless shocked by what she hears. Reluctant to concur, she insists that, 'Poverty is a great Evil, but to a woman of Education & feeling it ought not, it cannot be the greatest', adding, 'I would rather be Teacher at a school (and I can think of nothing worse) than marry a Man I did not like.' Although the satiric touch about teaching is reminiscent of the early writings, the tone of the conversation is altogether more serious and suggests that its subject could not be kept entirely under comic control. The painful debate between two far from wealthy sisters about their possible futures was only too close to Jane Austen's own experience.

Emma Watson's resistance to the idea of pursuing a husband 'merely for the sake of situation' suggests a degree of anger at the predicament of women whose adult lives depended entirely on their ability to attract a sufficiently well-heeled man. Nor is her objection countered by her sister's wishful thinking – 'I think I could like any good humoured Man with a comfortable Income.' The difference of opinion points clearly to Jane Austen's views on the matter, which would be spelled out with unequivocal clarity ten years later, when she counselled her niece, Fanny Knight, in November 1814, against any thought of marriage, if she were still harbouring doubts about her own feelings: 'Anything is to be preferred or endured rather than marrying without Affection.' Despite the pressures so graphically portrayed in 'The Watsons', where the need to secure a future home and husband turns Emma's sisters into desperate rivals, Jane Austen believed firmly that no one should marry without love. She had no illusions, however, about the difficulties facing those unlucky enough to be forced into the pursuit of love and failing to find it. The story she began after completing *Northanger Abbey* addressed a problem that she would revisit imaginatively throughout her life.

Jane Austen was a single woman living in a rented house with her sister and parents when she wrote 'The Watsons', but she could have been a wife and the mistress of a country mansion in Hampshire. Two years earlier in 1802, she had accepted a proposal of marriage from Harris Bigg-Wither, younger brother of her close friends, Catherine and Alethea Bigg. She was staying with the Bigg sisters at Manydown Park, on the way back from seeing Edward in Kent, when Harris, whom she had known since childhood, took the opportunity to ask Jane to marry him. She said 'Yes' at once, but by the very next morning she had changed her mind. Why? The most likely explanation is that she spent a very restless night agonising over her decision, and came to the conclusion that she was not in love with Harris and was never likely to be. No amount of fondness for him, or for his sisters, could compensate for the absence of real, passionate love. He might be a good companion, he might inherit a wonderful estate only a few miles from Steventon, but she knew that it was better to remain a spinster, with a limited income and without a permanent home, than to marry without the deepest emotional attachment. Her later advice to Edward's daughter, Fanny Knight, was founded on personal conviction.

In 1802, Jane Austen was probably still hoping to fall in love with someone who might turn out to be her future husband. Even if Marianne Dashwood considered a woman of twenty-seven to be well past the age when she might hope to inspire affection in a man, Jane Austen knew that plenty of people found romantic fulfilment beyond their early twenties. Eliza had not married Henry until 1797, when she was thirty-six. Whether Jane Austen suffered from the kind of feelings attributed to Elizabeth in 'The Watsons' ('A heart wounded like yours can have little inclination for Matrimony'), is not known. Her early flirtation with Tom Lefroy has attracted a great deal of attention in recent years, inspiring a book, a film and an enormous amount of speculation. The evidence relating to her emotional life, however, is frustratingly sparse. As so often, the known facts are interesting enough to generate lively imaginative interpretations, but insufficient to establish any full, authoritative account of crucial moments in her life. It seems just as possible that Jane Austen was in love with someone whose name has never been identified in the nineteenth-century recollections, nor by later admirers. Or she may have had a sequence of secret passions whose details were wisely kept from her extended family and which would hardly have survived in her letters.

Very little is known about who she met during the years after the move from Hampshire. Though based in Bath, the Austens had holidays in Devonshire, Dorset and Sussex, admiring the scenery, swimming in the sea and, inevitably, attending parties in the fashionable seaside resorts. Long after Jane Austen's death,

Cassandra admitted to their niece, Caroline, that her sister had fallen in love with a 'very charming man' ('I never heard Aunt Cass speak of anyone else with such admiration')[21] whom she met on one of their summer visits to the coast. Apparently, they planned to continue seeing each other after the Austens went back to Bath, but the man, whose name remains a mystery, had died soon afterwards. If this experience belonged to the first summer trip to Sidmouth in 1801, it may have had a bearing on Jane Austen's initial confusion over Harris Bigg-Wither's proposal. It may have altered her emotional life and general outlook for ever. But equally, it may not.

The impressions of Jane Austen that emerge from the early recollections suggest a person whose uneventful life remained largely untroubled by romantic entanglements and whose devotion to her family and her writing was completely absorbing. Nevertheless, Henry Austen, James Edward Austen-Leigh and Caroline Austen all describe her as a very attractive woman. Her brother's account, written within months of his sister's death, describes her graceful way of moving, her fine complexion, her sweet voice and the delightfully expressive face, which displayed so openly 'that cheerfulness, sensibility, and benevolence, which were her real characteristics'.[22] Her nephew's memories, though recorded half a century later, seem just as warm: 'In complexion she was a clear brunette with a rich colour; she had full round cheeks, with mouth and nose small and well formed, bright hazel eyes, and brown hair forming natural curls close round her face'.[23] Although he considered Aunt Jane less 'regularly handsome' than Aunt Cassandra, he was alert to her special attractions – 'her countenance had a peculiar charm of its own to the eyes of most beholders'. Such a woman would hardly have failed to attract admirers, and Caroline was clear that her aunt was 'established as a very pretty girl, in the opinion of most of her neighbours'.[24] Jane Austen enjoyed parties and she met plenty of men – perhaps she cared for none of them? With no direct account of Jane Austen's private feelings, we can do nothing but speculate.

What is certain, however, is that when she represented the processes of love and courtship in her mature novels, she was able to capture the feelings of her heroines with unprecedented literary skill. It is hard to imagine a writer who had never been in love succeeding in conveying Marianne Dashwood's sufferings with such care and sympathy, nor depicting the overwhelming joy felt by Anne Elliot at the end of *Persuasion*. Throughout her mature fiction, the mysterious effects of love and desire are explored with an understanding that enables readers to respond to the heroine's emotional twists and turns as if she were a real person. Jane Austen's generous treatment of misconstrued attentions or misplaced affection may result entirely from acute observation of those around her, but it seems unlikely. We may not have any definitive revelatory statement in a journal, or even in her private letters, but Jane Austen left the evidence of her deep personal knowledge of the human heart in every one of the novels she published.

Jane Austen may have abandoned 'The Watsons' because it was addressing issues that might have seemed too close to her own situation, or she may have been too distracted by a packed social diary and the frequent holidays and trips to visit family and friends. It is also possible that as a serious writer, she knew that her story was just not working. The non-publication of 'Susan' cannot have helped stimulate renewed creative energy, and there were plenty of other reasons for sinking into low spirits. Mrs Austen's anxieties about her own health, which had often been something of a trial to her daughters ('she sometimes complains of an Asthma, a Dropsy, Water in her Chest & a Liver Disorder'), had become a real cause for concern since the onset of a more dangerous illness.[25] Although she recovered from the attack, the comic verse she wrote to celebrate, paradoxically, reveals its seriousness: 'Says Death, "I've been trying these three weeks or more / To seize an old Madam here at Number Four"'.[26] Death may have been disappointed on this occasion, but now that Mrs Austen was in her sixties the possibility that things might turn out differently next time was only too real.

Mrs Austen may have encouraged the family to laugh in the face of death, but there were situations where even the most advanced sense of humour was powerless to help. Hastings' death in October 1801 at the age of fifteen brought grief not only on account of the boy himself, but also because of the thoughts it prompted about Jane's elder brother, George, who had suffered from fits in his childhood, so much like those that had afflicted Eliza's unlucky son. Three years later, Jane Austen's twenty-ninth birthday was darkened by the news that Mrs Lefroy had been killed suddenly, when her horse bolted during a routine shopping expedition to Overton. The extraordinary accident brought back painful memories of Jane Cooper's early death in a crashed carriage in 1798. But the worst was still to come. Within a month of Mrs Lefroy's fall, Jane Austen's father was dead.

Jane wrote at once to tell her brother, Frank, describing the suddenness of their father's decline into 'fever, violent tremulousness, & the greatest degree of Feebleness'. For once, all her comic energy was suspended. The comfort offered to her brother, whose shock she so thoughtfully anticipates, gives a rare insight into Jane Austen's own ultimate source of strength and consolation: her faith in her father's intrinsic goodness and his 'constant preparation for another World'. During the harrowing hours of his illness, Jane had joined her sister and her mother in fervent prayers for his release from suffering, and in the aftermath she was similarly sustained by her faith. Nevertheless, the magnitude of her loss and its practical effects on those left behind, cast a very dark cloud over her early thirties.

The death of George Austen left his widow and their daughters in difficult circumstances. They remained in Bath for about a year, in more modest accommodation in Gay Street, before moving to Southampton where Frank had set up home after his marriage to Mary Gibson in June 1806. When Frank went away to sea again the following year, his mother and sisters moved into his home, and stayed for the next two years. Although she had always been very conscious of Frank's naval career, living with his wife and helping care for their baby brought home the daily dangers of life at sea and the enormous relief of the Captain's shore leave. The years in Southampton, with Portsmouth nearby, gave Jane Austen her first experience of life in a major port, full of news about British engagements overseas and the progress of the war. She saw at first hand the great warships packed with men and cannons, the trading vessels and passenger boats, and the huge variety of people who filled the quayside. Southampton had its share of elegant buildings and balls, but the sense of purpose that galvanised so much activity at the harbour in Portsmouth offered a striking contrast to the leisurely and often ailing society of Bath. The last words of Jane Austen's last complete novel celebrate the domestic virtues and national importance of the British navy. Just as her earliest writings were meant as presents for her family, so she would eventually use her published works to pay tribute to those whose support had meant so much to her, and whose merits she regarded with such high esteem.

If Frank had rescued his mother and sisters from the in-securities of temporary lodgings by welcoming them into his growing household, it was Edward who eventually gave them a home of their own. His own life was shattered in 1808 by the sudden death of his wife, Elizabeth, a few days after giving birth. Cassandra was staying with the family at Godmersham when the devastating blow struck, leaving Edward inconsolable and eleven children without a mother. While Cassandra tried to comfort Fanny and her little brothers and sisters, the two eldest boys, who were at school in Winchester, went to stay with Aunt Jane in Southampton. A letter to Cassandra written on 24th October describes Jane Austen's efforts to divert their nephews with 'spillikins, paper ships, riddles, conundrums, and cards', but also makes references to their own 'plans'. By October 1808, Mrs Austen and her daughters were being given a choice between two of the smaller houses on Edward's estates, one in Kent and one in Hampshire. They plumped for Chawton, a few miles from Steventon, and over the next few months the plans turned into serious preparations.

The prospect of the move prompted Jane Austen into positive action. After years of wondering what had happened to 'Susan', she decided to write to Crosby on 5th April 1809 to ask whether they had lost the manuscript, signing her letter 'MAD' ('Mrs Ashton Dennis, Post Office, Southampton'). Her offer to replace it with another copy was answered curtly by Richard Crosby who informed her that his firm was under no obligation to publish the novel, but would take proceedings against any other publisher who did so. If she wanted to recover ownership of her work, she would need to reimburse Crosby with £10, the sum originally paid for 'Susan'. Although Jane Austen abandoned the matter for the time being, her decision to get to grips with a situation that had been in unsatisfactory suspension for six years suggests a renewed sense of determination and a reviving optimism about her writing. Once safely installed at Chawton, with a home of her own, Jane Austen began work on another novel. 'Susan' was currently imprisoned in a publisher's vault in London, and Emma Watson was abandoned, but there were other stories that had been drafted more than ten years before. 'Elinor and Marianne' came out of the cupboard and started to take on a new life, just as their author was doing.

Whatever Jane Austen had imagined for the two sisters in the middle of the 1790s could now be developed with far greater depth because of her experiences over the intervening years. Her new novel provided an opportunity to deal with the painful questions of parental death and expulsion from the family home, and although so many details concerning the Dashwood family were quite different from her own, the circumstances that now propelled the plot were things that Jane Austen knew about from first hand. Her fictional account of Mrs Dashwood and her daughters being offered a cottage on the estate of a wealthy

relative has an obvious connection to personal events. The brief description of the Dashwoods' new home in Devonshire being a 'comfortable and compact' house, though 'defective' as a cottage, would have fitted Chawton Cottage, with its square brick frontage, just as well.

The glimpse of the daughters 'endeavouring, by placing around them their books and other possessions, to form themselves a home', also allows an insight into Jane Austen's idea of what was most important to turn unfamiliar surroundings into a home. She had had plenty of experience of placing books and other possessions into new rooms over the last eight years, but settling into Chawton Cottage had an air of permanence. After the restless years in Bath and Southampton, with the numerous journeys to other towns and other people's houses, the Austen sisters had come to a halt in a small country village not very far from the one where they had grown up. It was a new stage of life, but it was also a return to something deeply familiar. Just as William Wordsworth was finding the rediscovery of his child-hood home in the Lake District enormously reinvigorating, so Jane Austen's return to Hampshire provided the stimulus for the extraordinary creative outpouring of the next eight years.

The Author of *Sense and Sensibility* and *Pride and Prejudice*
1809–13

The first conversation between Elinor Dashwood and Colonel Brandon in *Sense and Sensibility* explores the benefits and disadvantages of gradual maturity. Jane Austen had begun to use fictional dialogue as a way of presenting opposing views of important issues in *Northanger Abbey* and 'The Watsons', and now she developed the technique in the novel she began to revise on her return to Chawton. When Elinor expresses her hopes that 'a few years' will modify her younger sister's romantic notions and 'settle her opinions on the reasonable basis of common sense and observation', Colonel Brandon replies with surprising warmth, 'No, no, do not desire it, – for when the romantic refinements of a young mind are obliged to give way, how frequently are they succeeded by such opinions as are but too common, and too dangerous!' The exchange is reminiscent of Henry Tilney's admiration for Catherine Morland's innocent enthusiasm for the pleasures of Bath, but in *Sense and Sensibility* it is complicated by the focus on Marianne Dashwood, and the relative ages of Elinor and Colonel Brandon. Instead of the case for experience and rationality being made by the middle-aged, well-travelled military man, it is being argued by a young woman only two years older than the girl whose opinions she so confidently regards as being among the childish things that must be put away. The scene reveals not only Jane Austen's maturing style, but also her awareness that growing older brought perils of its own. Elinor Dashwood might believe, from the advanced age of nineteen, that additional years inevitably brought good sense, but Colonel Brandon was able to voice the possibility that age might do nothing more than induce the commonplace.

For a creative writer, the thought that the idealistic or imaginative must inevitably be crushed by the rational and known, was not necessarily something to celebrate. Even less welcome was the possibility that the bright gleam of originality invariably faded into the light of common day. As Jane Austen re-read the work she had first conceived fourteen years earlier, she was confronted with hard questions about whether the intervening period had brought the advantages anticipated by Elinor or the limitations observed by Colonel Brandon. If her novel were to succeed, she needed to find a way of retaining its early energy while restraining its excesses. As her writing developed, Jane Austen recognised that there were different ways of creating original works of art, and that the skills acquired from experience and experimentation were ultimately as important as the initial sparks of inspiration behind the story. In *Sense and Sensibility*, however, the different elements that fuse with such powerful results in her mature fiction are seen as conflicting tendencies. Was imagination invariably at odds with reason? Impulsiveness with restraint? Sense with sensibility? The pain experienced by both the heroines, and by so many others in the novel, is indicative of the seriousness of a problem that was both artistic and moral. Jane Austen resolutely tackled the inherent difficulties of revising old work that somehow embodies a younger self and in the next work she prepared for publication, the mood is very much lighter and less troubled.

Although Jane Austen's early versions of the novel that became *Sense and Sensibility* have not survived, it is not difficult to see its connections with the unpublished works that were preserved. If it began life as an epistolary novel in 1795, then it probably had something in common with 'Love and Freindship', 'Lesley Castle' and *Lady Susan*. Marianne's farewell to Norland, her views on matrimony and the weather, her accident, rescue, romance, broken heart and near-fatal illness, might all have been conceived initially as a parody of contemporary sentimental fiction, like so many of Jane Austen's other pieces. When Laura and Sophia sigh and faint on the sofa in 'Love and Freindship', they are designed to make fun of the literature of sensibility, with its swooning heroines and tearful heroes. In *Lady Susan*, Jane Austen had taken a different approach to the topic by creating a protagonist who seemed to lack any capacity for sympathy at all, but recognised the ways in which her more sensitive acquaintances could be manipulated. The more realistic language and the excessive selfishness of the central character, however, were creating the path towards a more subtle kind of humour, in which feeling might be allowed a place. As Jane Austen turned from *Lady Susan* to 'Elinor and Marianne', her new epistolary experiment probably attempted not only a more realistic style of correspondence than that of 'Love and Freindship', but also a more sympathetic representation of her young heroines' emotions.

Whether 'Elinor and Marianne' consisted entirely of the correspondence between sisters is not known, but it is easy to see how, in a first draft, Lucy Steele might have been represented largely through her own inelegant prose, how Marianne's romance with Willoughby might have flourished and been cut off through secret notes, or how Colonel Brandon's past could have been revealed in a long letter. When Jane Austen initially revised 'Elinor and Marianne' in 1797–8, she may have introduced the distinctive narration also adopted for *Northanger Abbey*, and transformed most of the fictional letters into conversations. Whether she modified Marianne Dashwood's expressions of sensibility at that stage, however, seems unlikely. Since *Northanger Abbey* includes self-conscious parody of Gothic novels, it seems probable that the early alterations to 'Elinor and Marianne' would have been made to the narrative style and plot, but not the spoof sensibility. By 1809, however, Jane Austen had begun to find the agonies of disappointed love less comical, or at least more worthy of serious consideration.

Although the novel has often been read as a critique of the contemporary 'cult of sensibility', it would be a mistake to assume that Jane Austen herself was unsympathetic to Marianne Dashwood. Since the books most admired by Marianne were also favourites of Jane Austen's, she would certainly have scored highly on Marianne's litmus test for sensibility. Jane Austen's letters, however, especially those written at excruciating moments such as Elizabeth Austen's sudden death, suggest that she was also capable of exerting herself and concealing strong feelings in order to spare those of others, just as Elinor Dashwood does. When her elder brother James read *Sense and Sensibility*, he saw at once that both the Dashwood girls were based on his own sister:

> On such subjects no Wonder that she shou'd write well,
> In whom so united those qualities dwell;
> Where 'dear Sensibility', Sterne's darling Maid,
> With Sense so attemper'd is finely pourtray'd.
> Fair Elinor's Self in that Mind is exprest,
> And the Feelings of Marianne live in that Breast.[27]

The creation of an all-knowing narrator meant, however, that Jane Austen's own personality could wear a number of different masks in her fiction, and though both the Dashwood sisters may be self-portraits, they also work as independent creations and convincingly individual characters. The obvious contrast between them may derive from Jane Austen's own complicated internal divisions, but it also serves as a means to explore ideas from different angles, and to reveal underlying unities in the face of more serious opposition.

Though Elinor quickly emerges as a figure of self-control and a foil for Marianne's more outspoken attitudes, both sisters are characterised by their sensitivity. The ridicule of sensibility that many readers have perceived in the novel is rapidly modified by much stronger criticism of those characters who lack any feeling for others: Marianne's passion for dead leaves has its comical aspect, but is still vastly preferable to the savage behaviour of Fanny Dashwood. If the revised novel retains some of the early jokes about contemporary literary trends, it is sustained by serious concern about the conventions governing a society that prided itself on politeness. Despite the humorous surface, there is an underlying current of anger running through the scenes in which the open feelings of a healthy, seventeen-year-old girl are condemned as rude or unacceptable. Jane Austen's frustration over the suffering of young women at the hands of their friends and relations is nowhere more apparent than in *Sense and Sensibility*, even though the novel carries an overt warning against unguarded emotional confessions. Elinor's inclination to conceal the truth may prove to be wise counsel, but only because the Dashwood sisters are surrounded by self-seeking or insensitive characters who abuse their trust.

Rather than endorse the social codes that prove so stifling to Marianne's spirit, the novel criticises the hypocrisy of a society that seems civilised but in fact offers little support to its more vulnerable members. Its sense of the injustices evident in everyday life and the way in which material success is not always enjoyed by the most deserving is apparent at once. After the death of Mr Dashwood, his daughters are ousted from their home by the unholy alliance of English inheritance law and their sister-in-law. The conversation may turn on gifts of china, but the actions being taken are brutal. The predicament of Mrs Dashwood and her three daughters makes an obvious comment on the dependency of wives, but this is itself qualified by the triumphant conquest of Norland which Fanny Dashwood accomplishes through her own marriage. Jane Austen had developed a form in which her own experience could deepen her fiction, because it was also tempered by rich knowledge of human society, drawn from years of careful observation. She knew very well that one family's misfortune often proved to be the making of another's prosperity, and that those on the way down were not necessarily spared further distress. Unlike so many of her contemporaries, however, she avoided a conventional presentation of suffering innocence, knowing that her story would carry greater conviction if the characters and their fortunes were more mixed, and their afflictions more like those within the experience of her readers.

Realistic portrayal of the problems confronting so many people also allowed for a kind of social comment that was profoundly felt, but free of the polemical tone that had seized so many novels in the Revolutionary decade of the 1790s. The pressure to marry which made the start of 'The Watsons' so uncomfortable is again evident in the Dashwoods' enforced removal to Devonshire and the embarrassing raillery to which they are then subjected at Barton Park. But it is countered by the devastating portrait of the Middletons, who fill their house with guests to dilute each other, or of Mr Palmer, who has been 'soured by finding, like many others of his sex, that through some unaccountable bias in favour of beauty, he was the husband of a very silly woman'. Marriage might be the cup awarded by contemporary society to successful young women, but Jane Austen was well aware that it sometimes proved, if not poisonous, then decidedly blighting. While some female characters in the novel gain great advantage from their marriages, others suffer years of dullness and even misery. As so often in her fiction, Jane Austen paints a society in which fortune seems fickle and human beings cope in different ways with the difficulties they suddenly find themselves facing. The problems are pervasive, but the means to tackle them are individual.

Despite its clear-sighted condemnation of individual shortcomings and prevailing social assumptions, however, the outlook of *Sense and Sensibility* is far from bleak. Some of those apparently introduced to try the patience of the heroines turn out to be their truest friends. Marianne's almost allergic reaction to Mrs Jennings, for example, is eventually shown to have been mistaken, while her quick judgement of Colonel Brandon and his flannel waistcoat is inverted completely. The negative portrayal of so many marriages is largely forgotten in the happiness that radiates from Elinor's eventual union, which transforms the potential tragedy of the novel into a traditional comedic conclusion. The new narrative style, with its sympathetic focus on the Dashwood sisters and their varying responses to the world, enabled Jane Austen to qualify points without sacrificing consistency.

Though far more restrained in tone than her anarchic early writings, *Sense and Sensibility* demonstrates a new kind of narrative freedom. In *Northanger Abbey*, Jane Austen had shown her interest in developing more convincing characters and a plot that could fully engage the reader, but in *Sense and Sensibility* she also allowed real emotion into her narrative. Readers are not only encouraged to see the funny side of her young heroines, but also to mind very much about what they are forced to endure: the suspense of the novel depends on imaginative involvement with their lives. The handling of Marianne's disappointment at discovering that the gentleman approaching on horseback is Edward Ferrars has a psychological acuteness that lifts the novel above mockery *and* sentimentality. Though still full of unresolved tensions, *Sense and Sensibility* is marked by Jane Austen's peculiar genius, and makes an astonishing debut for the published novelist.

Once Jane Austen had relaxed the parodic grip on her storytelling, she had no difficulty with finding a publisher. Although contemporary conventions prevented her from conducting her own business transactions initially, Henry was more than happy to act as her literary agent. He offered *Sense and Sensibility* to the London-based firm of Thomas Egerton and it was accepted at once. Although the agreement meant that Jane Austen would bear the production costs if the novel failed to sell, the risk turned out to have been well worth taking. *Sense and Sensibility* was published in October 1811, and immediately began to attract attention. Critical notices appeared in the press, and within three months of publication the novel was being enjoyed at Court, with no less prominent a reader than Princess Charlotte confessing to be amongst its admirers. Within two years, the first edition had completely sold out, making Jane Austen the handsome profit of £140. By that time she was hard at work on *Mansfield Park*, but in the meantime, Thomas Egerton had shrewdly offered to buy the copyright of the novel that had occupied her as soon as *Sense and Sensibility* was finished – *Pride and Prejudice*.

The confidence that came with publication shines out of every chapter of *Pride and Prejudice*. When it was finished, Jane Austen described her new novel as 'too light & bright & sparkling', but this hardly sounds like artistic failure.[28] Once *Sense and Sensibility* had been accepted and was making its way into print, Jane Austen turned her newly developed skills towards the old family favourite, 'First Impressions'. Rejections might eventually be regretted more profoundly by those who had made them than by those they had spurned, as Jane Austen's revisions made abundantly clear. Both Cadell and Crosby would come to rue their failure to spot the true value of works once submitted to their firms by the author of *Sense and Sensibility*. In *Pride and Prejudice*, hasty judgements and prolonged repentance are treated with all the exuberant humour of one whose own undervalued brilliance has at last been recognised. When Elizabeth Bennet is slighted by Mr Darcy at the Meryton assembly, her response is cheerfully resilient: 'She told the story however with great spirit among her friends; for she had a lively, playful disposition, which delighted in any thing ridiculous.' Her author's temperament was similarly playful, and after years of silence and insecurity she was now ready to turn painful experiences into funny stories, extending her circle to a vast audience of delighted admirers.

The extent of Jane Austen's revisions to 'First Impressions' is no more certain than the transformation of earlier versions of *Northanger Abbey* and *Sense and Sensibility*. She admitted in a letter to Cassandra that she had 'lopt and cropt' the story, but there are also references to her 'writing', which suggests fresh composition. The atmosphere of the novel captures the mood of the earlier letters, when Jane was in her twenties and describing her triumphs and disappointments on the dance-floor, which accords with its origins in 1797. It is not unlikely, however, that as she revised the story in 1811–12, she re-read some of the letters preserved by her sister, and incorporated the memories prompted by the details. Representation of the balls in *Pride and Prejudice* may owe something to the Steventon Christmas Ball of 1798, for example, where Jane remembered 'Mr Calland, who appeared as usual with his hat in his hand, & stood every now and then behind Catherine & me to be talked to & abused for not dancing'. If this suggests that Elizabeth Bennet was a portrait of the author's younger self, however, it is important to notice that as the letter continues it begins to sound more like Lydia: 'We teized him however into it at last; – I was very glad to see him after so long a separation, & he was rather the Genius & Flirt of the Evening.' Jane Austen not only had the draft of a novel, but also a stash of letters and personal experience to furnish her with the materials for her next book. Most important of all, however, was the knowledge that it was the *next* book – that she was an author whose work mattered.

In *Sense and Sensibility*, Jane Austen seems to be exploring a series of conflicts that have to be resolved in secrecy, but in *Pride and Prejudice* everything opens up. Where Elinor's caution about revealing feelings had been endorsed by the course of the narrative, Jane Bennet's proves almost disastrous. Mr Darcy's failure to expose Wickham's character means that Lydia and her family are unprepared for his predatory behaviour, while Darcy's own clumsiness in expressing emotion results in many pages of mortification. The openness of *Pride and Prejudice* is very different from that of *Sense and Sensibility*, however, for Elizabeth's outspoken wit offends only those characters whose outlook already seems inadequate. Unlike Marianne, whose impulsiveness has such unhappy consequences, Elizabeth behaves spontaneously and wins the immediate admiration of those who matter. Both heroines run, but where Marianne symbolically slips and falls, Elizabeth crosses 'field after field at a quick pace, jumping over stiles and springing over puddles'. Nothing deters her, and the novel celebrates the success of a woman whose refusal to be cowed or uncomfortably confined leads eventually to personal happiness. In *Sense and Sensibility*, everything seems very difficult, but *Pride and Prejudice* exults in its own sense of possibility.

Though so much lighter in tone than its predecessor, *Pride and Prejudice* is not without the same social concerns and sympathies, however. Again the precarious situation of contemporary women is evident, but the iniquities of a system of male inheritance are now treated with comedy, by making it a subject 'on which Mrs Bennet was beyond the reach of reason'. Her husband's laconic recitation of the letter from his cousin, Mr Collins ('who, when I am dead, may turn you all out of this house as soon as he pleases'), shows that the Bennet daughters are no more secure than the Dashwoods, but it also reassures readers that in such a good-humoured novel nothing very distressing is likely to take place. Even when Charlotte Lucas accepts a husband for whom she can have little feeling because, at twenty-seven, she needs a 'comfortable home', the potential misery is diffused by the force of Jane Austen's fine comic touches. When Elizabeth visits the married couple, the more painful aspect of her perceptive observation is balanced by the wit of its expression: 'When Mr Collins could be forgotten, there was really a great air of comfort throughout, and by Charlotte's evident enjoyment of it, Elizabeth supposed he must be often forgotten.' There is an additional joke, however, in the very idea that Charlotte's new husband could ever be forgotten.

Mr Collins, along with Mrs Bennet and Lady Catherine de Bourgh, provide an exuberant kind of entertainment quite distinct from the quick wit of Elizabeth and her father, or from the embarrassing situational comedy of the Bennet family, or from the satirised speeches of Sir William Lucas and the Bingley sisters. Their attitudes are exaggerated almost to the point of caricature, but the interaction with less extravagant creations keeps them within the realms of credibility and thus crucial to the success of the narrative. Despite its varied cast, no character in the novel seems to be introduced purely as a comic interlude. *Pride and Prejudice* is controlled with great care, as character after character enters at just the right moment to fulfil a crucial role in the overall design.

The witty, conversational tone of the novel's narrator keeps the story firmly grounded in the matter-of-fact and, as a result, Jane Austen is able to draw on the comedies she had seen performed first at home in Steventon and later in the professional theatres of Bath, London and Southampton. She had learned to love figures like Mrs Malaprop and Sir Lucius O'Trigger in her childhood, and now had the confidence to create characters whose comic magnificence would excel those of Sheridan by emerging so startlingly from the pages of a realistic novel. The kind of dialogue that propelled *The Rivals* or *The School for Scandal* could also be adapted for *Pride and Prejudice*, if only the characters' voices could be distinguished sufficiently. With scenes that depicted five sisters at home, the need to create lines that were both convincingly natural and instantly recognisable was paramount. Elizabeth commands attention by her lively conciseness ('Compliments always take *you* by surprise, and *me* never'), to which her elder sister provides the perfect foil. Lydia, as the youngest daughter, competes by using slang-words ('Lord!') and mentioning the names of officers, while Kitty is reduced to coughing and exclamations. Mary, 'the only plain one in the family', has to rely on her determined accomplishments, and interrupts conversations with either a long quotation from a moral essay or an even longer concerto. Each daughter is easily identifiable through her speech and in *Pride and Prejudice*, Jane Austen developed her skills in characterisation by adapting the techniques of the stage to her endlessly flexible pages.

The boldness of her new novel was not confined to its artistic innovations, however. In addition to the delightfully irreverent heroine, whose general attitudes provide such a refreshing contrast to the kind of models promoted in the contemporary educational manuals for girls, Jane Austen presented her readers with a story that involves abductions and extra-marital sex. The worst fears of eighteenth-century moralists are realised in the behaviour of George Wickham, but far from following the literary convention of condemning either the rake or his victims, Jane Austen rescued both Georgiana and Lydia from social disgrace and punished Wickham with nothing harsher than a silly wife.

Unlike Richardson's novels, the focus of *Pride and Prejudice* is not on the seduction of the younger girls, but rather on the embarrassment of their elder sisters. As with the comic containment of Mr Bennet's threatened demise, there is never any real sense that Lydia's elopement will lead to her destruction, but the distressing effects of her rash actions on the rest of the family are examined with great sensitivity. Despite its effervescent humour, *Pride and Prejudice* is just as concerned with the feelings of its heroines whose contrasting responses to their changing circumstances lie at the heart of the novel. Readers may laugh at the novel's dazzling line-up of comic turns and marvel at the brilliant observations of human interactions; they may admire the skilful construction of the plot and the beautifully turned sentences from which it is made; they may be provoked into deeper consideration of the flaws in English society or the evasive wartime setting of the novel; but everyone who enjoys *Pride and Prejudice* will be compelled by the central narrative. Though Mrs Bennet's now famous assumption that 'a single man in possession of a good fortune must be in want of a wife' is relentlessly mocked throughout, there can be few readers who remain immune to the intense satisfaction of the final union. *Pride and Prejudice* has many facets, but like *Sense and Sensibility* it is essentially a love story. Unlike its immediate predecessor, however, *Pride and Prejudice* is prepared to offer the possibility of unreserved happiness.

Mansfield Park and *Emma*
1813–15

The intensity of Jane Austen's preoccupation with her writing cannot be overstated. Although her nephew's recollections conjure up a picture of the modest aunt quickly putting aside her writing at the sound of approaching visitors as if producing tea and conversation were every bit as important to her as creating such a scene on paper, her own letters tell a different story. A sisterly enquiry about the progress of *Sense and Sensibility* provoked an unusual metaphor – 'No indeed, I am never too busy to think of S&S. I can no more forget it than a mother forget her sucking child'.[29] It recurs two years later to express Jane's excitement over the arrival of *Pride and Prejudice*: 'I want to tell you that I have got my own darling Child from London.' The comments jump out from the correspondence as rare revelations of genuine feeling, unmasked by irony, self-deprecation or comic absurdity. Jane Austen was referring to her novels as her children. By now, she was a single woman approaching forty, so the likelihood of having a baby of her own was remote. Instead of children, Jane Austen was producing books, and the affection with which she talks about the characters of *Pride and Prejudice* in letters to Cassandra demonstrates that the emotional satisfaction she derived from writing was profound.

Although Jane Austen never experienced motherhood, she maintained a deep interest in education and the ways in which children might be affected by their upbringing. Edward's large family provided an endless topic for her mother, while James and Frank's children, who lived much nearer Chawton Cottage, were frequent visitors. Her eldest nieces, Anna Austen and Fanny Knight (whose name had changed in 1812 when Edward inherited his estate), were now the same age as the Dashwood sisters and the Bennets, so she had plenty of opportunity for seeing the trials of adolescence and early adulthood at first hand. As Jane Austen watched her nephews and nieces growing up, she was also reminded of her own childhood and alerted to the contrasts and the continuities between younger and older selves. Had she changed? Had Cassandra? Or James? Or any of her siblings? What made people grow into the adults they became? How important were their physical surroundings or material possessions? Were personalities fixed from birth, or did the combined influence of education, family, place and income determine a child's character? Or was it the result of an individual's unique experiences?

These were questions that had already occupied many of the greatest minds of the past century and continued to attract vigorous debate, but Jane Austen's approach was always imaginative rather than philosophical, her mind moved by the human dimensions of a question. When she read essays, she responded passionately to their authors, even if the subject was as unpromising as Captain Pasley's *Essay on the Military Policy and Institutions of the British Empire* ('I am as much in love with the Author as I ever was with Clarkson or Buchanan', she wrote on 24th January 1813). When she considered political or theoretical ideas they rapidly changed into the conversations and behaviour of her imaginary creations. As a girl, her history lessons had provoked intense involvement with injured queens and indignation over detestable monsters. Now, her imagination was under tighter control, but the capacity to translate dry fact and argument into compelling human drama remained. The primary concern of her novels was the creation of believable human beings in a beautifully structured fictional world. By the time she

wrote *Mansfield Park*, however, she knew that her acute observations of human behaviour might be conveyed in such a way that larger questions could also be addressed in fiction.

In 1812, with the contract for *Pride and Prejudice* agreed, Jane Austen was bursting with ideas for her next novel. Rather than reach into her treasure trove of older writings to retrieve 'Lady Susan' or 'The Watsons', she embarked on an entirely new story which would allow her to explore questions of education, family relationships and the different kinds of lives forced on individuals by their birth and background. It was not that she had abandoned the imaginative stocks of her earlier years, but instead of revising work written twenty years before, she drew on her memories of Steventon and Southampton, and visits to numerous English country houses. She was still interested in sisters, but now her attention turned from the necessity of marriage to its consequences, as she imagined the contrasting households of the three Miss Wards. Charlotte Lucas' wry observation that 'Happiness in marriage was entirely a matter of chance' is tested in *Mansfield Park* through the cameo portraits of the three sisters and their relative successes – Maria's captivation of Sir Thomas Bertram, her elder sister's subsequent marriage to the Reverend Norris, and Frances' impulsive secret wedding with Lieutenant Price, a low-ranking officer in an unelevated branch of the Navy. Two have married for love, but while one lives a life of easy luxury, the other is worn down by frequent pregnancies and the struggle to maintain a large family on a low income. The economic and social divisions of contemporary society, which had furnished *Pride and Prejudice* with a rich seam of jokes about snobbery, upward-mobility and the erotic charge of a good estate, were now providing the framework for a novel whose tone was far less 'light & bright & sparkling'. Frances Ward pays a heavy price for her unlucky infatuation, and her married name is a constant reminder of her mistake.

Jane Austen was far too thoughtful a writer to be content with presenting any straightforward equation between material comfort and happiness, however, and as the schematic opening chapter leads into the more capacious surroundings of Mansfield Park, initial judgements are qualified by the complexity of the narrative and its focus on the next generation. The transplantation of a child into an unfamiliar environment had always been a sensitive issue for the Austen family, and so Jane's decision to remove Fanny Price from her home in Portsmouth perhaps recalled painful memories of Edward's adoption by the Knights and George's permanent exile as well as her own school experiences. As she recreated the intense unhappiness of the displaced child, lost in the vast grandeur of her uncle's great house, however, she was also breaking new narrative ground, shifting rapidly between profound sympathy for the vulnerable heroine and satirical comment on the unattractive figures who surround her. Fanny Price may not be able to defend herself, but the narrator is well equipped to demolish her oppressors with a caustic aside.

Despite the unsentimental attitude to Frances Ward's misguided romance, it quickly becomes apparent that the comfortable upbringing enjoyed by her elder sister's children has done nothing to ensure their personal well-being. One of the central ironies of the novel is that Mrs Price's apparently disastrous choice has nevertheless resulted in the birth of Fanny, William and Susan, who are all presented as far more admirable characters than their spoiled cousins. If Austen avoided equating wealth and goodness, however, neither was she endorsing Sir Thomas' final realisation of 'the advantages of early hardship and discipline, and the consciousness of being born to struggle and endure'. Sir Thomas' second son, Edmund, has turned out well even without the advantages his father suddenly identifies as key to the integrity of the young Prices. It is evident by the closing chapters that the older generation have been just as much in need of sound education as their children and that much of the unhappiness depicted in the novel has resulted from irresponsible parenting. Henry Crawford has been 'ruined by early independence and bad domestic example', while Julia Bertram's marginal superiority to her sister has resulted from her being 'less the darling' of Mrs Norris, 'less flattered, and less spoiled'.

Although *Mansfield Park* is clear about the unfortunate consequences of spoiling children, it also demonstrates that there are no easy answers to the question of what constitutes a good education or a good person. Despite the obvious sympathy for Fanny as a victim of bullying relations, she has not proved as universally appealing as Elizabeth Bennet, whom Jane Austen herself pronounced to be 'as delightful a creature as ever appeared in print'.[30] Many readers have balked at the seriousness of Fanny and Edmund, their embarrassment over naughty jokes or amateur dramatics, and the understated nature of the final declaration. Fanny's mounting horror at the noise levels in her own parents' home, her relief at returning to the tranquillity of Mansfield Park, despite its many flaws, and her disapproval of so many of the residents and their guests, have not helped to endear her to readers already disappointed by her lack of wit and energy. In *Mansfield Park*, however, Jane Austen was marking out new territory as a novelist. She was no longer limited to the close family audience, who expected to be delighted, and could therefore experiment with a different kind of fiction. In her next novel, she deliberately created a heroine whom 'no one but myself' would much like, but the idea of discomforting her readers was already well developed in *Mansfield Park*.[31]

As a mature novelist, Jane Austen felt no need to use her work as a vehicle for submerged autobiography, even though she drew from the rich store of memories she had garnered over the years. The theatricals gain conviction from her early experience of the rehearsals at Steventon, but the chapters also fulfil many roles in *Mansfield Park*. They develop the plot by introducing new characters and revealing different aspects of those already in place, while also offering a sophisticated exploration of the nature of art and the ways in which a play can become part of a novel. The major themes of class, education and personal choice are also highlighted, as soon as Edmund has expressed his reservations about fashionable private productions by 'a set of gentlemen and ladies who have all the disadvantages of education and decorum to struggle through'. Whatever Jane Austen's own experience, the theatricals are a beautifully crafted episode, intricately connected to numerous threads in the novel. In her skilled hands, the raw material of personal experience was turned into fine art.

Similarly, references to William Price's promotion and the various ships in Portsmouth owe much to Frank and Charles Austen's naval careers, but this does not mean that the Navy is included for the sake of family interest alone. William's wide experience of the world provides another comment on the disadvantages of gentlemen, most explicit when an eager account of his hazardous profession prompts Henry Crawford to a rare moment of self-knowledge: 'The glory of heroism, of usefulness, of exertion, of endurance, made his own habits of self indulgence appear in shameful contrast; and he wished he had been a William Price.' Jane Austen was paying a private tribute to her own brothers in her portrait of William, but she was also making more ambitious points about the contemporary class structure, systems of inheritance and personal responsibilities to society. The careful contrasts between those in the Navy and those born into wealth gradually make plain that *Mansfield Park*'s concern with economics is national as well as domestic.

Questions about the proper use of riches had attracted writers throughout the eighteenth century, but took on a new urgency in relation to the French Revolution and the more immediate Regency crisis. By 1813, when Jane Austen was writing *Mansfield Park*, the extravagance of the Prince Regent was legendary. Tales of his lavish parties and building projects startled his subjects, especially since many were struggling for survival by working very long hours in appalling conditions. There was even concern during the long war with France that while the Prince indulged in six-course banquets, the nation's food supply was actually running out, leaving the poor starving. At the same time, the recent campaign to abolish the slave trade had raised public awareness that part of Britain's prosperity had depended on the cruellest exploitation of human beings. Though patriotic loyalty was accentuated by Napoleon's alarming conquests abroad, doubts about the nation's internal wellbeing were widespread.

Although Jane Austen's novels with their carefully realised domestic settings seem largely untroubled by the great issues of her day, it is evident from comments in her letters that she was extremely concerned about the human aspects of contemporary political questions. Her dislike of the Prince Regent, for example, was expressed most clearly in her sympathy for the Princess of Wales ('Poor Woman! I shall support her as long as I can, because she *is* a Woman, & because I hate her Husband'), while her warm interest in the abolition of the slave trade is evident in her 'love' of the campaigner, Thomas Clarkson.[32] *Mansfield Park* avoids conversations about contemporary politics, but in its imaginative exploration of the rights and wrongs of private economies it addresses questions of intense public concern. When Fanny Price asks her uncle about the slave trade on his return from Antigua her question is answered by silence, even though her relations are happy to discuss the fashionable topics of landscape gardening, home improvements or the delivery of sermons. Jane Austen allowed nothing improbable, nothing contrived into her new novel, but nevertheless developed ways of suggesting that the realistic details in her text were also signs of much broader concerns. Sir Thomas' 'recent losses on his West India Estate, in addition to his elder son's extravagance' were, after all, anxieties of which George III might have complained in his more lucid moments, while the discussions over whether alterations to an ancient inheritance should involve massive destruction or mere modification applied as much to the British Constitution as to Mr Rushworth's house at Sotherton.

Mansfield Park is not a political novel in the sense that its purpose is polemical, or its action allegorical, but in the careful detail and thoughtful construction of contrasting characters, it demonstrates the ways in which a novel could offer numerous satisfactions. Like *Sense and Sensibility* and *Pride and Prejudice*, it had a strong plot, brilliant comic observation and sympathetic involvement with characters in realistic settings, but it also provided a new forum for testing contemporary ideas in action. The high ideals of the modern novel set out in *Northanger Abbey* were rapidly being realised.

Jane Austen's interest in the economic basis of society was undoubtedly sharpened by her own circumstances. Unlike the Bertram daughters, she had not been born into a wealthy, landed family even though many of her friends and relations had inherited estates. After her father's death, Jane Austen had spent years in rented houses and remained dependent for a home on the charity of her brothers. The success of her novels gave her an income for the first time in her life and with it, renewed self-confidence and a different angle on the very idea of independence. In *Mansfield Park*, she had focused on the figure of the poor relation, but in her next novel she explored similar questions of wealth, power, responsibility, education and the accidents of birth from the perspective of the wealthy. The very first line introduces Emma Woodhouse, 'Handsome, clever, and rich.' It is almost as if Fanny Price has been displaced by Maria Bertram.

Even before readers arrived at chapter one, *Emma*'s distinction from the earlier novels was apparent from the new publisher – the fashionable firm of John Murray – and the surprising dedication to 'His Royal Highness, the Prince Regent'. *Emma* was clearly receiving the best treatment because, like the heroine, it could not put up with any other. Despite the confidence exuded by her new novel and despite the example set by Murray's most famous author, Lord Byron, however, Jane Austen did little to exploit her own chance to become a literary celebrity. *Emma* was dedicated to the Prince Regent not because Jane Austen wanted to flatter the future King, but because he had declared himself an admirer. All her novels had been published anonymously, but by the time *Mansfield Park* appeared her authorship was widely known. Henry, especially, found it difficult to keep quiet when he heard his sister's books being discussed, as Jane reported to Frank: 'Henry heard P.&P. warmly praised in Scotland, by Lady Robt. Kerr and another Lady; – & what does he do in the warmth of Brotherly vanity & Love, but immediately tell them who wrote it!' She was torn between dismay that the great secret, once out, would never be contained again, and delight in Henry's obvious pride in her success, 'A Thing once set going in that way – one knows how it spreads! – and he, dear Creature, has set it going so much more than once. I know it is all done from affection and partiality.' Since Henry had lost Eliza to cancer only a few months before, Jane was prepared to forgive him anything, but she was more grateful to Frank for his respect for her own wishes. Public recognition was not an unmixed blessing, as she discovered when summoned to Carlton House by the Prince Regent's librarian. She could hardly refuse to dedicate her novel to the future King once he had decided to bestow royal patronage, but those closest to her smiled at the sight of the grand flourish, remembering her earlier, decidedly parodic dedications. No doubt the author-ess enjoyed the irony of attracting royal patronage for a novel set more firmly than any of the others in a quiet corner of the kingdom.

Emma is a novel of rural retirement, in which London, Bath and Richmond are mentioned only as distant destinations of characters disappearing from centre-stage. Unlike the peripatetic heroines of her previous books, Emma remains at home and travels only a few miles in the entire course of the narrative. Of all Jane Austen's heroines, however, Emma Woodhouse is the least retiring. *Mansfield Park* had begun by emphasising the range of characters contributing to the narrative, but *Emma* concen-trates from the first on its heroine. Although she is a younger sister like Elizabeth Bennet or Marianne Dashwood, Emma dominates her novel in an entirely new way, and much of the narrative is conveyed through her confident, but often mistaken perception of those around her. The novel is concerned with relative fortunes and examines the issue of female dependency through the portrayal of Harriet Smith, Jane Fairfax, Mrs Weston and Miss Bates, but the imaginative focus is on Emma Woodhouse, whose personal wealth means that she is free of the economic obligation to marry that had influenced so many of Jane Austen's earlier characters. 'I have none of the usual inducements of women to marry,' she tells Harriet, 'Fortune I do not want; employment I do not want; consequence I do not want; I believe few married women are half as much mistress of their husband's house, as I am of Hartfield.' Emma's eloquence on the subject is as startling to readers of Jane Austen's earlier novels as it is to Harriet Smith. She is an entirely new kind of heroine and has unsettled readers ever since her first appearance in December 1815.

Despite Emma's sense of her own independence, she is nevertheless as preoccupied with the question of marriage as any of her predecessors. It is just that she does not restrict the matter to her own future. The novel opens on the evening of her governess' wedding, which Emma takes personal pride in having brought about ('I made the match, you know'). Within a couple of chapters, she has begun directing her match-making skills towards Harriet Smith, whose sequence of infatuations and disappointments provides one of the main strands of the narrative. Emma's determined search for prospective husbands for Harriet and denial of her own attraction to men shows Jane Austen's acute insight into the psychology of displaced desire, and much of the comedy and ultimate satisfaction of the novel arises from Emma's apparently endless misunderstanding, but eventual recognition, of her true feelings. The combination of the heroine's abundant self-confidence and unerring capacity to misread situations provides a new kind of comedy in which the witty woman can also be the butt of many jokes.

Jane Austen had already made much of the comic potential of the match-maker in *Pride and Prejudice*, but Mrs Bennet's energy is contained within set dialogues and situations, her thoughts visible only from her speeches. Emma, however, has the freedom to create her own romances and the will to extend her managerial powers into the lives of all those around her. At times, she is almost like a novelist within her own novel, as she conjures up suitors for Harriet and ignores the reality of her friend's situation, attractions and feelings. She is proud of being an 'imaginist', ever ready to be 'on fire with speculation and foresight', and so the slightest information rapidly assumes dramatic significance in her eager mind. Minor incidents are magnified and preserved in Emma's imagination, and her desire to turn life into fiction is apparent in the constant recital of 'the story of Harriet and the gipsies'.

If *Northanger Abbey* had considered the relationship between reading fiction and interpreting immediate experience, *Emma* extended the field to explore the very nature of imaginative creation. Jane Austen's perennial enjoyment of playing with literary convention was emerging in far more subtle ways, with the elaborate Gothic parody of the past condensed into passing jokes about Emma's fear of Miss Bates 'haunting the Abbey'. Her interest was now focused not so much on how to write successful fiction (a problem she had already solved), but on the very sources and processes of creative thought. By developing a narrative technique that allowed readers to share the heroine's perspective on a scene even without the help of dialogue, Jane Austen was able to represent the workings of Emma's mind with far more complexity than she had afforded to her characters before. At times she offered Emma's thoughts as direct internal speech ('"There is no charm equal to tenderness of heart" said she afterwards to herself'). At other moments, she developed the brilliant free indirect style that allowed the omniscient narrator to recede and Emma's thoughts to take over, almost imperceptibly ('Emma, beginning hastily and with an arch look, but soon stopping – it was better, however, to know the worst at once – ').

The novel's focus on the heroine also allows for detailed development of the growth of consciousness, so readers are able to trace the progress of such things as the 'ingenious and animating suspicion' that enters Emma's brain after an offhand remark by Miss Bates about her niece's friendship with the Dixons. As the idea is nourished by Jane Fairfax's subsequent reticence and Frank Churchill's interest, the imagined tendresse becomes more real to Emma than much of what is actually going on before her eyes. Jane Austen's attention to the stories that take hold of Emma's mind in this way affords remarkable insight into the imaginative process. Emma does not read the world through her library books like Catherine Morland, but her imaginative response is just as powerful, and often as misleading. Since Emma's sources lie not in the Gothic novels of two centuries ago, but in her immediate circle, she is a character to whom everyone can relate and whose mistakes are inevitably shared. For while many readers see through her confusions over Mr Dixon at once, few avoid responding with some impatience to Miss Bates's long speeches and, as a consequence, are almost as thrown by discovering the limitations of their own judgement as Emma after the visit to Box Hill.

If Emma's imagination leads to mistakes, however, it is also what makes her such a life-affirming character. Her father's habit of offering only very small portions of the plainest food to his guests is countered by Emma's generous spirit and her 'pleasure in sending them away happy'. Her sense of independence and her imaginative freedom enable her to make gifts and generate happiness, even if her attempts are not always sufficiently attentive to alternative views. Emma's relish for life means that she possesses a rare capacity for contentment, and the little scene in Highbury where she waits for Harriet to choose her muslin demonstrates that the benefits of her imagination far outweigh any of the drawbacks: 'when her eyes fell only on the butcher with his tray, a tidy old woman travelling homewards from shop with her full basket, two curs quarrelling over a dirty bone, and a string of dawdling children round the baker's little bow-window eyeing the gingerbread, she knew she had no reason to complain, and was amused enough'. In a situation that might have nothing to interest the Bertrams or the Crawfords, Emma is perfectly happy. Anything can provide the materials for a new story, as long as the onlooker has a mind to create.

In *Emma*, Jane Austen was celebrating the power of the human imagination, and demonstrating the riches of a rural environment. If her earlier novels had made jokes at the expense of Lady Susan or Caroline Bingley, with their prejudices against country towns and villages, *Emma* defended provincial life by revealing its untold imaginative wealth. Gilbert White, whose best-selling *Natural History of Selborne* was published in 1789, had already shown the world that his tiny Hampshire village, only four miles from Chawton, was a place of unique importance. Jane Austen similarly presented Highbury as the hub of the world, but her remarkable achievement lay in creating a fictional place every bit as complete and convincing as her neighbour's record of his parish. Frank Churchill may joke about becoming a 'true citizen of Highbury' by buying gloves at Ford's, but his gently patronising tone is roundly answered by Mr Knightley's contempt for a man who would travel all the way to London for a haircut. Mr Knightley's relief at riding home after staying on in London, 'vigorously, day after day' is a telling inversion of the kinds of metropolitan prejudice encountered by Jane Austen on her visits to Henry in Chelsea. It may take time to understand the true value of Highbury, but many readers have discovered over the years that the world of *Emma* lives on in their minds with far greater vitality than many of the real places they have known.

Emma was not, after all, an inappropriate gift for the Prince. Its patriotism is apparent in the paean of praise to Donwell Abbey and the Abbey-Mill Farm: 'It was a sweet view – sweet to the eye and the mind. English verdure, English culture, English comfort, seen under a sun bright, without being oppressive.' What need was there to travel abroad, with such delights to be found on the doorstep? The hidden heart of England was open to anyone who took the time to stop and look. *Emma*'s celebratory tone undoubtedly owed something to the national sense of relief at Napoleon's defeat and the banishment of longstanding fears about a French invasion, but it also reflects Jane Austen's deep gratitude for the quiet countryside that had proved so congenial to her creative spirit. In a letter offering advice to James Austen's daughter Anna, who was writing a novel of her own in 1814, Aunt Jane congratulated her on setting the scene in 'such a spot as is the delight of my life; – 3 or 4 families in a Country Village is the very thing to work on'. It was the very kind of spot where she was now happiest because she knew it worked so well, and therefore she could too. In *Mansfield Park*, she had examined the idea of a true home, but in *Emma* she knew that she had found one and her happiness fills the novel.

Emma may be a flawed heroine, and at times her 'solitary grandeur' makes her seem melancholy despite all the blessings of her existence, but the novel is infused with a deep satisfaction. It is Jane Austen's most complicated creation, with a huge cast of brilliantly realised characters and a host of minor figures whose presence contributes to the overall sense of completion. The varied comedy of misunderstanding and game-playing, of eccentricity and prejudice, of snobbery and hypochondria, of misplaced affection and rejected addresses, is woven into a fine structure that is at once extraordinarily intricate and strong. Everything is so perfectly placed that it seems to follow as naturally and inevitably as the seasons, despite the complexity of the plot. Emma's vital freedom is possible *because* her world is so carefully grounded. Jane Austen was demonstrating the importance of attending to the tiniest parts as well as to their essential and cumulative contribution to the larger entity. As a healthy example for the future King of England, *Emma* could hardly have been better.

Persuasion
1816

In *Emma*, Jane Austen had resolved so many of the problems she had set for herself that she inadvertently created a new one: what could she write next? Such a virtuoso performance was not easy to follow, even for a writer whose voice had now achieved its perfect pitch. Once her authorship became known, she began to receive ideas from admirers such as James Stanier Clarke, the Prince's librarian, who wrote on 16th November 1815 to suggest that she might turn her talents to delineating 'the Habits of Life and Character and enthusiasm of a Clergyman – who should pass his time between the metropolis & the Country – who should be something like Beatties Minstrel'. Although she politely demurred from the task, claiming that she might be equal to the 'comic part of the Character... but not the Good, the Enthusiastic, the Literary', Mr Clarke continued to send suggestions and by December, he was even imagining the Clergyman being sent to sea 'as the friend of some distinguished Naval Character about a Court'. When he wrote again in March, urging her to compose a 'Historical Romance illustrative of the august House of Cobourg', it was time to make herself plain: 'I could not sit seriously down to write a serious Romance under any other motive than to save my Life', she replied, '& if it were indispensable for me to keep it up & never relax into laughing at myself or other people, I am sure I should be hung before I had finished the first Chapter.' She did not send Mr Clarke the hilarious 'Plan of a Novel' which his well-meaning, but ill-judged ideas had provoked.

Although Jane Austen modestly stressed her literary limitations and incurably comic inclinations, the correspondence with the Prince Regent's household displays the same underlying confidence that shines from every line of *Emma*. 'No – I must keep to my own style & go on in my own Way', she wrote and even though the letter is dated 1st April 1816, she clearly meant what she said. It was the very day that she wrote to John Murray, thanking him for sending her a copy of the *Quarterly Review* which carried a long critical discussion of her work by no less a master than Walter Scott.

An author who was receiving serious public praise in one of the most influential literary journals had no need of advice on the subject of her next book, however well intended. She had spent long enough doubting the success of her work and lost out on the copyright of *Pride and Prejudice* as a result. With the publication of *Emma*, she had found a new publisher and better terms, so she was not going to resume any deferential attitude. Indeed, in the early months of 1816, she had had the satisfaction of recovering the old manuscript of 'Susan' from Crosby, and revealing the identity of its anonymous author just as the *Quarterly* put its seal on her fame. By now Jane Austen was not prepared to publish work unless it met the exceptionally high standards that she had achieved in *Emma*, however, and so although she went back to 'Susan', renaming her novel 'Catherine' and making various related alterations, she was no longer satisfied with her earlier work. In March 1817, she wrote to her niece, Fanny, admitting that 'Miss Catherine is put upon the Shelve for the present, and I do not know that she will ever come out'. The same letter nevertheless reveals in confidence that she had, after all, been working with much greater success on another project: 'I have a something ready for Publication, which may perhaps appear in about a twelvemonth hence.' The 'something' was *Persuasion*.

Although Jane Austen had begun working on the new novel soon after she completed *Emma* in March 1815, she had largely managed to keep her work quiet. It had been a year of upheavals, with Napoleon's last attempt to regain power and his defeat at Waterloo providing the remarkable international prelude to Henry's near-fatal illness in the autumn and the subsequent collapse of his bank. Henry's bankruptcy made a great impact on the entire family, not only through their natural sympathy for his distresses, but also because Frank was also a partner in the bank and so the financial repercussions for everyone were considerable. Charles was still far away in the Eastern Mediterranean, but seemed to take his share in the family misfortunes when his ship was wrecked in a storm in the Aegean. Though exonerated from all blame, Charles came home depressed and poor, and took years to recover professionally from the disgrace of losing a ship. Worst of all, though not recognised as such at the time, Jane's health was beginning to decline. She began suffering from a bad back and deep fatigue during the summer of 1816 and, despite cheerful references to her recovery in letters throughout the next winter, she was evidently aware that something was not right.

The national rejoicing that accompanied the end of the war was evident in the buoyant mood of *Emma*, but by 1816 it seemed to be giving way to an all-engulfing depression. Nevertheless, in between attending to Henry in his London sickbed, supporting her mother through the family trials and entertaining the extended family during their numerous visits to Chawton, Jane Austen succeeded in writing a novel every bit as innovative as *Emma*. Although she had told Mr Clarke that she must keep to her own style, this did not mean repeating her earlier successes. In *Persuasion*, she reconsidered many aspects of her previous novels, but the result was something quite unlike any of them.

With its West Country setting and initial focus on the loss of the family home, *Persuasion* is reminiscent of *Sense and Sensibility*, though the later section in Bath, perhaps influenced by the recovery of the manuscript from Crosby, has more in common with *Northanger Abbey*. The opening chapters, with their satirical portrayal of Sir Walter Elliot, also recall the embarrassing parents and exaggerated comic characters of *Pride and Prejudice*. Sir Walter's daughters have reached the age at which Charlotte Lucas deemed it prudent to accept Mr Collins, and so the pressure to find a husband which afflicts so many of the female characters before Emma, is once again under scrutiny. At the same time, the interest in a Baronet's household, his extravagant expenditure and the effect of external influence on domestic decisions, seem more like *Mansfield Park*, especially since aristocratic assumptions about the world are so clearly contrasted with those of the Navy. The symbolic transfer of Kellynch Hall from a flawed Baronet to a capable naval commander seems a natural development from *Mansfield Park*, and as Lieutenant Price's noisy house is replaced by the admirable domesticity of Captain Harville and Admiral Croft, Jane Austen was extending her affectionate tribute to Frank and Charles, just when they needed it most.

If *Persuasion* reconsiders almost every major theme from the earlier novels, however, it is most indebted stylistically to *Emma*. *Persuasion* is a personal book in the way that none of the others are, but its private quality is achieved through the intense concentration on the mind of the heroine. In *Emma*, Jane Austen had developed ways of presenting the narrative largely from the perspective of the central character, creating passages in which Emma's thoughts dominate the narrative interest and even restricting much of the novel's dialogue to the subject of Emma. *Persuasion*, too, moves rapidly from the external portrayal of Sir Walter and his selfish obsessions, to the secret inner life of his middle daughter. Anne Elliot may be disregarded by her family, but to readers what goes on in her mind is far more compelling than what comes out of her father's mouth. The drama in *Persuasion* is mental, and the entire novel reflects the peculiarly sensitive interior of the heroine. Where Emma's thoughts are often quick and decisive, reflected in short sentences, broken by dashes and exclamation marks, Anne Elliot's restrained contemplation is represented by long, beautifully controlled sentences that can run on for ten lines at a time. Even the passages of more detached narration retain an affinity to Anne's perception by adopting similar sentence patterns:

> They were come too late in the year for any amusement or variety which Lyme, as a public place, might offer; the rooms were shut up, the lodgers almost all gone, scarcely any family but of the residents left – and, as there is nothing to admire in the buildings themselves, the remarkable situation of the town, the principal street almost hurrying into the water, the walk to the Cobb, skirting round the pleasant little bay, which in the season is animated with bathing machines and company, the Cobb itself, its old wonders and new improvements, with the very beautiful line of cliffs stretching out to the east of the town, are what the stranger's eye will seek; and a very strange stranger it must be, who does not see the charms in the immediate environs of Lyme, to make him wish to know it better.

This striking paragraph carries all the conviction of first-hand experience, and is obviously drawn from Jane Austen's memories of holidays in the Dorset resort in 1803 and 1804. Though the detail impresses the reality of the place on the page, its muted tone conveys the thoughtfulness of retrospect, of someone who understands what it means to feel that she has come too late. The bathing machines Jane Austen had used when she spent all day swimming in the little bay were packed away, and the impulse to retrieve them imaginatively – to relive remembered pleasures – was checked by the cool knowledge that that time was past, and all its aching joys were now no more. *Persuasion* nevertheless demonstrates the abundant artistic recompense derived from acknowledging the very difference.

Though much indebted to the innovations of *Emma*, reflective passages such as the description of Lyme distinguish *Persuasion* from the earlier novels, while also showing that the very process of reconsidering them paved the way to new achievement. When Jane Austen observed that 'these places must be visited, and visited again, to make the worth of Lyme understood', she was writing from her own experience – not just of Lyme itself, but of intense imaginative visiting and recollection. After completing *Emma*, she was revisiting her personal and literary past. *Persuasion* is at once nostalgic and experimental, its unique character arising from the perpetual interaction between the sense of then and now, and the quiet, though often painful, reflection on the changes.

Persuasion is the first novel in which Jane Austen makes the past a crucial part of her narrative, impressing its importance from the opening chapter. Sir Walter Elliot's obsession with his family tree and Elizabeth Elliot's 'consciousness of being nine-and-twenty', with thirteen years of presiding over Kellynch Hall behind her, prepare the way for the real focus of the novel: Anne's preoccupation with her own unhappy history. At twenty-seven, Anne is older than any of the heroines in the earlier novels and unlike her predecessors, her character has been formed by experiences that are not narrated directly. Where Emma has enjoyed her teenage years, with very little to distress or vex her, Anne Elliot's have been marked by loss and loneliness. The successive blows of her mother's death and her broken engagement have taken place before the moment when the novel begins, and so the narrative is perpetually gazing backwards at the months of intense happiness as well as the prolonged grief that occupies so much of Anne's internal experience.

Where *Emma* is kept entirely free of dates, *Persuasion* announces the dates of birth of the principal characters on the first page, and is then so specific about their ages that it is very clear to readers that the action of the novel takes place in 1814. The 'short period of exquisite felicity' enjoyed by Anne in the company of Captain Wentworth took place in 1806, a summer made all the more golden by its contrast with the surrounding years of warfare. Though Jane Austen had made passing references to public events in her previous novels, she had never before set the lives of her fictional characters so firmly against the great dramatic backdrop of her own turbulent times. Anne Elliot's sufferings were of a kind that anyone bereft and broken-hearted might experience, but they achieve a greater intensity through the additional fears relating to the international conflict. When her fiancé left the country after their engagement was ended, he was going off to a war in which his chances of survival were very uncertain. If *Emma* had caught the joyful mood of the moment of national peace, *Persuasion* reflected on the long years of anxiety which had gone before.

Although Jane Austen allowed her pen to dwell on feelings of misery in a way that she had never done before, however, the most remarkable aspect of *Persuasion* is its almost imperceptible change of mood. If at the beginning of the novel, Anne Elliot seems virtually paralysed by the distressing burden that has weighed on her for so many years, by the end she is staggered by 'an overpowering happiness'. The satisfaction of the novel's conclusion is greatly enriched by the sensitivity with which the heroine's feelings have been traced from dull depression, through moments of extreme pain, to a dawning capacity for amusement and a slowly recovering self-confidence, until the possibility of hope seems real again at last. The scene at the White Hart, which Jane Austen carefully rewrote after rejecting the first ending she had conceived, is perhaps the most powerful emotional moment in her entire oeuvre. It is certainly one of the most complicated and sophisticated chapters, with its extraordinary control of a roomful of characters engaging in different conversations, each of which carries additional resonances for Anne and Wentworth, though they do not exchange a word. In the end, Jane Austen reverted to the device she had loved as a girl – the fictional letter. But where in her youth she had invariably made fun of the written declaration and made her epistles a medium for parody, she now allowed Captain Wentworth to compose the most passionate address without a trace of irony. At forty, it seems, Jane Austen was prepared to lay down her comic defences when the situation demanded, and allow un-alloyed feeling to burst out across the page. No wonder Anne Elliot is stunned, and those around her seem momentarily at a loss.

Persuasion is barely two-thirds of the length of *Emma*, and yet its slim form contains the greatest extremes of emotion, the most striking contrasts in narrative tone, the widest spectrum of social classes, the longest sweep of time and the most ambitious connections between the domestic and the national of any of the novels. Though most concise in its dealings with minor char-acters, it is the most generous in its development of the heroine. Though the most preoccupied with location, it also seems the most displaced of all. For though each of the earlier novels sent their heroine on a significant journey, they also allowed her to return home, enlightened by her travels. In *Persuasion*, when Anne returns to Kellynch, she realises that her home has 'passed into better hands than its owners', and recognises that her expul-sion is permanent.

It is only as she begins to look forward rather than backwards, however, that the hints of an internal transformation can be fully realised. Once she has revisited Kellynch, and seen that the world is not contained there, but lies all before her, Anne is ready to be restored to her true self. She learns from the past, but is liberated from its more restrictive influence, and prepared to embrace new life wherever it might take her. The openness of Anne Elliot's future, in comparison with the carefully located heroines of the earlier novels, is entirely consistent with the flexi-bility of *Persuasion*. She may be without her familiar habits and circle, but in her new freedom, she is intensely happy. Jane Austen, too, had discovered hidden strengths in the course of writing *Persuasion*, and as she put down her pen in July 1816, seemed poised for future greatness. The emotional honesty of the book is such, however, that it also succeeds in conveying a dim sense that the happiness being celebrated so warmly is a kind of wishful thinking.

Winchester Races
1817

Jane Austen had no illusions about mortality. By 1817, she had seen the lives of two first cousins, three sisters-in-law, her sister's fiancé and her cousin's husband all cut short in their prime. She had lost her father, and had mourned the deaths of aunts and friends. Her letters are scattered with references to stillbirths and miscarriages, to mothers who died in labour and to children who succumbed soon afterwards. She had nursed both her mother and her elder brother through illnesses that nearly carried them off, and was even now hoping for an end to the suffering of her little niece, Harriet, whose mysterious brain disease was driving Charles Austen to distraction. In her novels, however, death is never described directly, and figures largely as a plot device to bring about an enabling change for the surviving characters. There are moments when death seems uncomfortably close – in Marianne Dashwood's sick chamber, at Mansfield Park during Tom Bertram's fever, on the hard stone of the Cobb in *Persuasion* – but in each case it is warded off, the mood lightens and the story continues. Much of the time, illness provides comedy: Mrs Bennet's nerves and Mr Woodhouse's worries are there to make us laugh rather than cry. As Jane Austen's own symptoms became more severe, she might have decided to abandon her writing and rest. Instead, she embarked on a new novel that satirised contemporary medicine.

In *Persuasion* she had recalled the Dorset shoreline with remarkable passages of lyrical beauty, but in *Sanditon* the sea-breezes are more biting. The little Sussex village that has suddenly been 'planned & built, & praised & puffed, & raised... to a Something of young Renown' by Mr Parker could hardly be more different from the wistful evocations of Lyme Regis.[33] The cool comment on the fleeting nature of fame encapsulated in Mr Parker's regret over his choice of 'Trafalgar House' for his new establishment ('for Waterloo is more the thing now') seems to anticipate the spirit of Byron's new poem *Don Juan* rather than to recall 'Tintern Abbey'. In *Persuasion* the satire had broken open to reveal the romantic yearning within, but 'Sanditon' even in its fragmentary form, reveals little sign of deep emotion beneath the rapid conversations about bilious attacks and rheumatism. In *Emma*, the relative merits of South End and Cromer are debated in the brilliant comic scene in which Mr Woodhouse and John Knightley are each determined to demonstrate the superiority of their own doctor. Now the medical humour was much less subtle, shooting out in Mr Parker's ludicrous enthusiasm for Sanditon's fresh air and deep water: 'They were antispasmodic, anti-pulmonary, anti-septic, anti-bilious & anti-rheumatic. Nobody could catch cold by the Sea. Nobody wanted Appetite by the Sea, Nobody wanted Spirits, Nobody wanted Strength.' The very things that Jane Austen most wanted, in fact, were being offered as hollow promises in the determinedly comic novel she was struggling to write. Even Sir Edward Denham's very funny attempts to seduce Charlotte by quoting Burns are poignantly ironic, since Burns himself had died of the fever developed after he attempted to cure himself of a rheumatic illness by bathing in the Solway Firth. Beneath the comedy runs the knowledge that whatever energy, money or hope human beings might invest in medical treatment, they would always be confronted in the end with the truth of their own mortality. Even when Mr Parker is at his most persuasive, his enthusiasm is quietly punctured when he announces that sea air and bathing 'nearly infallible'.

In letters written during the early months of 1817, Jane Austen maintained the same resolutely cheerful front, reassuring Fanny that she was 'tolerably well again, quite equal to walking about & enjoying the Air', but all the time, her health was failing. By May, the apothecary in Alton had given up on attempting to cure the violent attacks and overwhelming exhaustion that had seized her, and so Mr Lyford, a first-class surgeon from Winchester, was called to Chawton. Since it is clear, with hindsight, that she was in the grip of either Addison's disease or some form of cancer, any improvement could only be a temporary respite. What the Austens saw, however, was what they wanted to see – that Mr Lyford had worked wonders and 'gradually removed the Evil'. Jane must therefore go to Winchester to continue receiving his care. Her old friends, Elizabeth and Alethea Bigg, who were now living in the Cathedral Close, found a pretty house in College Street where the Austen sisters could stay until Jane recovered. 'I am now really a very genteel, portable sort of an Invalid', she observed in May, when faced with the prospect of being bumped along the sixteen-mile journey by carriage. But still she maintained her faith that 'the Providence of God' had restored her to better health, adding with a characteristic blend of wit and humility, '& may I be more fit to appear before him when I *am* summoned, than I shd have been now!'

The house overlooked the Headmaster's garden at Winchester school and through the bow-window she could hear the shouts of schoolboys. Across the street at the front was the great grey wall of the Close, built of flints and meant to last for ever. The chimes from the massive cathedral helped to order her prayers and calm her spirits. Although the doctors continued to be encouraging, Jane Austen knew well that her condition was serious and was making appropriate preparations. She had made a will in April, several weeks before the move to Winchester and apart from a few small gifts, she left everything to her 'tender, watchful, indefatigable nurse', Cassandra.[34] When she thought of what she owed her sister and 'to the anxious affection of all' her beloved family, she confessed, 'I can only cry over it, and pray to God to bless them more.' Six weeks after expressing these feelings, she had another attack which left her barely conscious. She died two days later, at half past four in the morning of Thursday, 18th July 1817.

For Cassandra, Jane's death was devastating: 'She was the sun of my life', she wrote, three days after her death, 'it is as if I had lost a part of myself.' The funeral, attended by Edward, Henry, Frank and James's eldest son, James Edward, took place early on Thursday, 24th July in order to be over by the time the first service began in the Cathedral. The sense of loss that convulsed her family is preserved on the large black tombstone in the floor of Winchester Cathedral, which states that 'their grief is in proportion to their affection' and that 'they know their loss to be irreparable'. The moving inscription speaks of 'The benevolence of her heart, the sweetness of her temper, the extraordinary endowments of her mind' and the 'warmest love' she inspired in those closest to her. But it makes no mention of her writing.

Although the monument seems to represent the final statement, the last words composed by Jane Austen herself adopted a rather different tone. Three days before she died, she dictated a poem to Cassandra. By now her mind was on the Cathedral, the tombs and the prayers, the vaulted ceilings and the arching aisles, the shrine of St Swithin behind the High Altar. Rather than compose a devotional lyric, however, Jane Austen's imagination was playing on the old legend of St Swithin's Day – if it rains on 15th July, it will rain for forty days afterwards. The story had its origins in St Swithin's canonisation, which took place on 15th July 971, and meant that his bones were moved from the old grave outside to a new shrine within the Cathedral. As Jane Austen lay dying on St Swithin's Day, 1817, she noticed that Winchester Races were taking place that very day, and was struck by what 'the old Saint' might think of the fashionable parade at the race meeting. Though her body was weak, her mind was still capable of imaginative leaps, as she described St

Swithin, springing from his shrine to address the Winchester race-goers from the Cathedral roof:

'Oh! Subjects rebellious! Oh Venta depraved
When once we are buried you think we are gone
But behold me immortal! By vice you're enslaved
You have sinned and must suffer, then farther he said

These races and revels and dissolute measures
With which you're debasing a neighbouring Plain
Let them stand – You shall meet with your curse
   in your pleasures
Set off for your course, I'll pursue with *my* rain.

Ye cannot but know my command o'er July
Henceforward I'll triumph in shewing my powers
Shift your race as you will it shall never be dry
The curse upon Venta is July in showers—'.[35]

Jane Austen's last work, characteristically enough, is a comic poem about the English weather.

Afterlife

'Behold me immortal!' When Jane Austen imagined St Swithin's refusal to lie down and be forgotten, she probably did not feel so confident about her own long-term survival. Despite the contemporary success of her work, the novel was still regarded in 1817 as a relatively minor genre, and not yet as serious literature. But during the nineteenth century the novel grew in stature and so did Jane Austen's standing as a writer. Despite the incomprehension of readers like Charlotte Bronte, her novels continued to be enjoyed and increasingly to attract a powerful body of influential admirers. For George Henry Lewes, the well-known writer, editor, reviewer and partner of George Eliot, there was no question of Jane Austen's work being forgotten, as he announced to readers of *Blackwood's Magazine* in 1859: 'Such art as hers can never grow old, can never be superseded.'[36] His prediction has proved true. By the end of the century, Jane Austen's novels were appearing in numerous editions, often beautifully bound and illustrated, while the foremost critics of the day were describing her as the Shakespeare of English prose. There were even special words for her supporters, and the *Oxford English Dictionary* records the use of 'Janeite' as early as 1896, with 'Austenite' and 'Austenian' being coined in the early twentieth century, as the numbers devoted to her work and memory continued to grow.

Interest in Jane Austen's own life had been stimulated initially by the brief, but affectionate 'Biographical Notice' written by her brother, Henry, to accompany *Northanger Abbey* and *Persuasion*, which were published together a few months after her death. He revised the short account when the novels were brought out as a set in 1833, but it was not until 1870 that the first substantial biography appeared, written by James Austen's son, James Edward Austen-Leigh, who had attended his aunt's funeral in 1817 and now felt a duty to collect any surviving family memories and compile a suitable tribute. *A Memoir of Jane Austen* stimulated renewed interest in the novels, especially when it reappeared in 1871 with fresh material, including the startling tale of 'Lady Susan'. Despite introducing Victorian readers to the unabashed amorality of Lady Susan, the *Memoir* also established a clear image of the novelist herself – as a retiring maiden aunt, living quietly with her mother and sister in a tiny country village. As critical interest in Austen's work became more serious, the popular idea of Jane Austen's rural England, filled with pretty girls in pretty dresses, and of a life untroubled by anything more difficult than the choice of dress or dancing partner, began to take root. The enduring appeal of Austen's work to numerous readers found permanent form a century after her death when, amid the devastation of the First World War, supporters from Britain and America commissioned a memorial tablet for Jane Austen's home at Chawton.

Soon after the war, R.W. Chapman began work on the first scholarly edition of Jane Austen's novels, which were published by Oxford University Press in 1923. Her status as a major author was now beyond doubt, and Chapman's edition provided a sound basis for the studies of her work and paperback editions that poured from numerous presses in the following decades. Jane Austen had the honour of being 'the first modern novelist' conferred on her by F.R. Leavis, whose confident judgements influenced a whole generation of younger scholars and writers. When Ian Watt published his seminal account of *The Rise of the Novel*, Jane Austen was singled out as the culmination of eighteenth-century experimentation and the inaugurator of the great English novel of the nineteenth century. At a time when women writers often seemed to be slipping out of critical sight, Jane Austen's reputation remained secure. As feminist critics in the 1970s and 80s began to challenge the male domination of the literary canon, Jane Austen, though hardly in need of rescue, received a wave of new attention from readers who especially admired her clear treatment of issues relating to women. Familiar assumptions about the novels were overturned by critics who saw a figure such as Emma Woodhouse not as a flawed heroine in need of careful correction, but as an icon of female empowerment. At the same time, sharpened awareness of the historical contexts in which Austen wrote meant that readers were more alert to issues such as slavery in *Mansfield Park*, or to the political implications of her estates, big houses and naval characters.

While academic debates have raged over Jane Austen's politics or lack of political awareness, the wider enthusiasm for her work has continued without abate. The development of film and television in the twentieth century provided an entirely new stage for Jane Austen's characters, who are now encountered by many people initially on screen rather than on the page. Aldous Huxley made the first adaptation of *Pride and Prejudice* for an MGM movie in 1940, while the BBC made a pioneering production of *Emma* in 1948. Jane Austen has remained a staple of television costume drama, but since the 1990s her novels have been transformed into a bewildering sequence of lavish adaptations, attracting the most celebrated actors, actresses and producers. In 1995 alone, Kate Winslet made her name as Marianne Dashwood in Ang Lee's film of *Sense and Sensibility*, Amanda Root gave a brilliant performance as Anne Elliot in Roger Michell's *Persuasion*, Amy Heckerling interpreted *Emma* for the cult teen movie, *Clueless*, while Andrew Davies' six-part adaptation of *Pride and Prejudice* fixed a dripping image of Mr Darcy in the minds of millions of viewers. The appetite for watching Jane Austen's stories seems unappeasable, and each year brings new versions to compete with those already in circulation.

Nor are film-makers content with adapting the novels. Jane Austen's life has also caught the imagination of audiences around the world, since it inspired *Becoming Jane* in 2007. James Edward Austen-Leigh and his sisters would probably have been surprised by the twenty-first century Hollywood response to their aunt, who is embodied in the beautiful form of Anne Hathaway and depicted in the grip of a mutual passion. The Jane Austen of contemporary imagination is youthful, confident and energetic, and as handy with a cricket bat as with a pen. She cuts quite a different figure from the late Victorian Miss Austen, with her neat little writing desk and her exquisite needlecraft. Each generation creates its idea of Jane Austen, who lives for ever in her own books. Two centuries have passed since her words were first heard speaking through the printed page of *Sense and Sensibility*. Far from becoming fainter with the passage of time, her voice, if altering at all, has grown stronger and clearer as the years have gone by.

Notes

1. *Jane Austen's Letters*, ed. Deirdre Le Faye, 3rd edn (Oxford, 1995), p. 336.

2. The principal sources of information concerning Jane Austen's family are the memoirs and recollections written by her relatives. See James Edward Austen-Leigh, *A Memoir of Jane Austen and Other Family Recollections*, ed. Kathryn Sutherland (Oxford, 2002); William Austen-Leigh and Richard Arthur Austen-Leigh, *Jane Austen: A Family Record*, ed. Deirdre Le Faye (London, 1989). For a more modern assessment of the Austen family, see George Holbert Tucker's useful book, *A History of Jane Austen's Family*, rev. edn (Stroud, 1998).

3. *The Complete Poems of James Austen*, ed. David Selwyn (Chawton, 2003), p. 20.

4. James Edward Austen-Leigh, *A Memoir of Jane Austen and other Family Recollections*, ed. Kathryn Sutherland (Oxford, 2002), p. 18.

5. Jane Austen, *Juvenilia*, ed. Peter Sabor, The Cambridge Edition of the Works of Jane Austen (Cambridge, 2006), p. 361.

6. Gilbert White, *The Natural History of Selborne*, ed. Richard Mabey (Harmondsworth, 1977), p. 265.

7. *Juvenilia*, p. 362.

8. ibid, pp. 3, 13.

9. ibid, p. 54.

10. ibid, p. 42.

11. ibid, p. 51.

12. ibid, p. 8.

13. ibid, pp. 343, 323.

14. ibid, p. 178.

15. ibid, p. 220.

16. ibid, p. 244.

17. 'Lady Susan', *The Works of Jane Austen: Volume VI, Minor Works*, ed. R.W. Chapman, rev. B.C. Southam (Oxford, 1969) p. 252.

18. Anna Lefroy, 'Recollections of Aunt Jane', in James Edward Austen-Leigh, *Memoir*, p. 158.

19. A.A. Mandal, 'Making Austen Mad: Benjamin Crosby and the non-publication of Susan', *RES*, ns 57 (2006), pp. 507–525.

20. 'The Watsons', Minor Works, p. 317.

21. Letter to James Edward Austen-Leigh, *Memoir*, p. 188.

22. Henry Austen, 'Biographical Notice of the Author', in James Edward Austen-Leigh, Memoir, p. 139.

23. James Edward Austen-Leigh, *Memoir*, p. 70.

24. Caroline Austen, 'My Aunt Jane Austen: A Memoir', in James Edward Austen-Leigh, *Memoir*, p. 169.

25. *Jane Austen's Letters*, p. 27.

26. The verse by Jane Austen's mother is published in full in W.R. and R.A. Austen-Leigh, *Family Record*, p. 125.

27. *Complete Poems of James Austen*, p. 39.

28. *Jane Austen's Letters*, p. 203.

29. ibid, p. 182.

30. ibid, p. 80.

31. Austen's assessment of Emma is recorded in James Edward Austen-Leigh's *Memoir*, p. 119.

32. *Jane Austen's Letters*, pp. 208, 78.

33. 'Sanditon', *Minor Works*, p. 371.

34. *Jane Austen's Letters*, pp. 339, 343.

35. The text is from Jane Austen, *Catharine and Other Writings*, ed. Margaret Ann Doody (Oxford, 1993), p. 246. Doody's introduction discusses the different surviving manuscripts of Austen's last poem, pp. xx–xxii.

36. G.H. Lewes, 'The Novels of Jane Austen', *Blackwood's Edinburgh Magazine* lxxxvi (July 1859), pp. 99–113.

Bibliography

A biography of this kind is inevitably indebted to the
numerous studies of Jane Austen's life and works. The list
below represents a selection of the most important sources.
Many of these books will be of interest to those who wish to
pursue their knowledge of Jane Austen beyond this brief life.
For the novels, it is best to read the texts in good editions with
helpful introductions and notes, such as those published in
the New Penguin series, Oxford World's Classics, Norton
Critical Editions or the Cambridge Edition of the Works
of Jane Austen.

Austen, Caroline, *Reminiscences of Caroline Austen*, ed. Deirdre Le Faye
    (Chawton, 1986).
Austen, James, *The Complete Poems of James Austen*, ed. David Selwyn
    (Chawton, 2003).
Austen, Jane, *The Novels of Jane Austen*, ed. R.W. Chapman (1923), 3rd edn,
    rev. Mary Lascelles, 5 vols (Oxford, 1965–1969.
—, *Minor Works (*from *The Works of Jane Austen: Volume VI, Minor Works)*,
    ed. R. W. Chapman, rev. B. C. Southam (Oxford, 1969).
—, *Juvenilia*, ed. Peter Sabor, The Cambridge Edition of the Works of
    Jane Austen (Cambridge, 2006).
—, *Jane Austen's Letters*, ed. Deirdre Le Faye, 3rd edn (Oxford, 1995).
Austen-Leigh, James Edward, *A Memoir of Jane Austen and other Family
    Recollections*, ed. Kathryn Sutherland (Oxford, 2002).
Austen-Leigh, William and Richard Arthur, *Jane Austen: A Family Record*,
    ed. Deirdre Le Faye (London, 1989).
Batey, Mavis, *Jane Austen and the English Landscape* (London, 1996).
Byrne, Paula, *Jane Austen and the Theatre* (London, 2002).
Copeland, Edward and McMaster, Juliet (eds.), *The Cambridge Companion
    to Jane Austen* (Cambridge, 1997).
Duckworth, Alistair, *The Improvement of the Estate,* new edn (Baltimore,
    1994).
Fergus, Jan, *Jane Austen: A Literary Life* (London, 1991).
Grey, J. David, Litz, W., and Southam, B. (eds.), *The Jane Austen Handbook*
    (London, 1986).
Harding, D.W., *Regulated Hatred*, ed. M. Lawlor (London, 1998).
Hill, Constance, *Jane Austen: Her Homes and Friends (*London, 1902*)*.
Honan, Park, *Jane Austen: Her Life* (London, 1987).

Hubback, J.H. and E.C., *Jane Austen's Sailor Brothers* (London, 1906).

Johnson, Claudia, *Jane Austen: Women, Politics and the Novel* (Chicago, 1988).

Lane, Maggie, *Jane Austen's England* (London, 1986)

—, *Jane Austen and Food* (London, 1995).

Le Faye, Deirdre, *A Chronology of Jane Austen* (Cambridge, 2006).

Leavis, F.R., *The Great Tradition* (London, 1948).

Litz, A. Walton, *Jane Austen: A Study of her Artistic Development* (London, 1965).

Lynch, Deirdre, ed., *Janeites: Austen's Disciples and Devotees* (Princeton, 2000).

Nokes, David, *Jane Austen* (London, 1997).

Sales, Roger, *Jane Austen and Representations of Regency England* (London, 1994).

Southam, Brian, *Jane Austen: The Critical Heritage,* 2 vols (London, 1968; 1987).

—, *Jane Austen and the Navy* (London, 2000).

—, *Jane Austen's Literary Manuscripts*, 2nd edn (London, 2002).

Spence, Jon, *Becoming Jane Austen* (London, 2003).

Tanner, Tony, *Jane Austen* (Basingstoke, 1986).

Todd, Janet (ed.), *Jane Austen in Context* (Cambridge, 2005).

Tomalin, Claire, *Jane Austen: A Life* (London, 1997).

Tucker, George Holbert, *A History of Jane Austen's Family*, rev. edn (Stroud, 1998).

Watt, Ian, *The Rise of the Novel* (London, 1957).

Wiltshire, John, *Jane Austen and the Body* (Cambridge, 1992).

Biographical note

Fiona Stafford is a Fellow of Somerville College and a Reader in English at the University of Oxford, where she regularly delivers lectures and tutorials on Jane Austen. Her editions of *Emma* and *Pride and Prejudice* appeared in 1996 and 2004, and she edited *Jane Austen: A Casebook of Criticism* in 2007. She has written essays on Jane Austen and many other writers of the Romantic period, and her books include: *The Sublime Savage: James Macpherson and The Poems of Ossian* (1988), *The Last of the Race: The Growth of a Myth from Milton to Darwin* (1994) and *Starting Lines in Scottish, English and Irish Poetry* (2000). She is currently writing a book about Local Attachments.

HESPERUS PRESS

Hesperus Press, as suggested by the Latin motto, is committed to bringing near what is far – far both in space and time. Works written by the greatest authors, and unjustly neglected or simply little known in the English-speaking world, are made accessible through new translations and a completely fresh editorial approach. Through these classic works, the reader is introduced to the greatest writers from all times and all cultures.

For more information on Hesperus Press, please visit our website: **www.hesperuspress.com**

ET REMOTISSIMA PROPE

SELECTED TITLES FROM HESPERUS PRESS

Brief Lives

Author	Title
Richard Canning	*Brief Lives: Oscar Wilde*
Patrick Miles	*Brief Lives: Anton Chekhov*
Melissa Valiska Gregory and Melisa Klimaszewski	*Brief Lives: Charles Dickens*

Classics, Modern Voices and New Fiction

Author	Title	Foreword writer
Jane Austen	*Lady Susan*	
Jane Austen	*Lesley Castle*	Zoë Heller
Jane Austen	*Love and Friendship*	Fay Weldon
Jane Austen	*The Watsons*	Kate Atkinson
Charles Baudelaire	*On Wine and Hashish*	Doris Lessing
Charlotte Brontë	*The Spell*	Nicola Barker
Miguel Cervantes	*The Dialogue of Dogs*	Ben Okri
Anton Chekhov	*The Story of a Nobody*	Louis de Bernières
Joseph Conrad	*The Return*	Colm Tóibín
Charles Dickens	*Mugby Junction*	Robert Macfarlane
Emily Dickinson	*The Single Hound*	Andrew Motion
George Eliot	*Janet's Repentance*	Kathryn Hughes
F. Scott Fitzgerald	*The Rich Boy*	John Updike
Gustave Flaubert	*November*	Nadine Gordimer
Yasmine Ghata	*The Calligrapher's Night*	
D.H. Lawrence	*Wintry Peacock*	Amit Chaudhuri
Katherine Mansfield	*In a German Pension*	Linda Grant
George Sand	*The Devil's Pool*	Victoria Glendinning
Ivan Turgenev	*Faust*	Simon Callow
Edith Wharton	*Sanctuary*	William Fiennes